Teaching Students to Dig Deeper

The Common Core in Action

Ben Johnson

EYE ON EDUCATION
6 DEPOT WAY WEST, SUITE 106
LARCHMONT, NY 10538
(914) 833-0551
(914) 833-0761 fax
www.eyeoneducation.com

Library of Congress Cataloging-in-Publication Data

Johnson, Ben.
Teaching students to dig deeper : the common core in action / by Ben Johnson.
   pages cm
  ISBN 978-1-59667-232-1
1. Thought and thinking—Study and teaching—United States.   2. Education—
Standards—United States.   3. College preparation programs—United States.
I. Title.
  LB1590.3.J645 2012
  373.73—dc23

2012032996

10 9 8 7 6 5 4 3 2 1

Sponsoring Editor: Robert Sickles
Production Editor: Lauren Davis
Copy Editor: Emily Goodman
Designer and Compositor: Dan Kantor
Cover Designer: Knoll Gilbert

Also Available from Eye On Education

Common Core Literacy Lesson Plans:
Ready-to-Use Resources, K–5
Lauren Davis, Editor

Common Core Literacy Lesson Plans:
Ready-to-Use Resources, 6–8
Lauren Davis, Editor

Common Core Literacy Lesson Plans:
Ready-to-Use Resources, 9–12
Lauren Davis, Editor

Teaching Critical Thinking:
Using Seminars for 21st Century Literacy
Terry Roberts and Laura Billings

Big Skills for the Common Core:
Literacy Strategies for the 6–12 Classroom
Amy Benjamin with Michael Hugelmeyer

Vocabulary at the Core:
Teaching the Common Core Standards
Amy Benjamin and John T. Crow

Vocabulary Strategies That Work:
Do This—Not That!
Lori G. Wilfong

Teaching Grammar: What Really Works
Amy Benjamin and Joan Berger

Rigor Made Easy: Getting Started
Barbara R. Blackburn

Rigor Is Not a Four-Letter Word, Second Edition
Barbara R. Blackburn

MEET THE AUTHOR

Ben Johnson enjoys being the Principal of Southside High School in San Antonio, Texas. He loves working with teachers, students, and parents in his calling as an educator. He has 28 years of experience in helping students and teachers to increase learning capacity. He has a masters degree from California State University at San Bernardino in Education Administration and he is in his last year as a doctoral student at the University of Phoenix. His dissertation is on the role of principals in promoting math and science teacher collaboration.

During his career, Ben Johnson has carried such auspicious titles as teacher, campus administrator, district administrator, university program manager, and private consultant. Like many educators, he has also adopted many other titles in "off times" in order to provide for his family. He began his career as a Spanish teacher and has never forgotten the important lessons he learned there:

- The mouth is connected to the brain and if the mouth is moving correctly, the brain is also.
- Students must have a reason to learn the language (or any thing).
- Students cannot be expected to remember something they cannot pronounce.
- The rule of three—students need at least three opportunities to learn for each concept.
- Total Physical Response and many other constructivist principles.

Ben is a strong proponent of Professional Learning Communities in schools. He is especially interested in helping teachers align their instruction to natural workings of the brain. Effective questioning, formative assessments, and technology are tools that help him do this. For Ben Johnson, the Common Core State Standards represent the liberation of teachers from worrying about what to teach so that they can focus more exclusively on how to teach it.

What little extra time that Ben has, he uses to be with his family in San Antonio, to be an Aggie Dad, and dote on his children and grandchildren. He stays active in his church and tries to keep physically fit in the swimming pool. Aside from his principal duties and studying for his doctorate, Ben also writes a biweekly blog for Edutopia.org.

SUPPLEMENTAL DOWNLOADS

Several of the figures discussed and displayed in this book are also available on Eye On Education's website as Adobe Acrobat files. Permission has been granted to purchasers of this book to download these resources and print them.

You can access the downloads by visiting *www.eyeoneducation.com*. From the home page, click on the Free tab, then click on Supplemental Downloads. Alternatively, you can search or browse our website for this book's product page, and click on "Log in to Access Supplemental Downloads."

Your book-buyer access code is **TSD-7232-1**.

Index of Free Downloads

CONTENTS

FOREWORD

Students are being pushed to go to college from the first day they enter kindergarten. Teachers struggling to provide relevance to what they are teaching frequently admonish students, "You will need to know this when you go to college!" Schools and school districts are "graded" by how many students are evaluated as college-ready. While each state has its own definition of what it considers to be "college-ready," the sad fact of the matter is that for all the hype about college-readiness, less than a third of the students graduating from high schools across the nation are able to meet even the minimum state college-readiness standards (Combs, Slate, Moore, Bustamante, Onwuegbuzie, & Edmonson, 2010).

In an effort to alleviate this situation, a state-based movement sponsored by the Council of Chief State School Officers and the National Governor's Association has created a set of Common Core State Standards (National Association of Governors and the Council of Chief School Officers, 2008). These standards are designed to help teachers, administrators, and education decision-makers—kindergarten to twelfth grade—prepare students to be college- and career-ready by the time they graduate from high school. The standards fall in two groups: mathematics and literacy. The literacy strand is further divided into three parts: Standards for English Language Arts & Literacy in History/Social Studies, Science, and Technical Subjects K–5; Standards for English Language Arts 6–12; and Standards for Literacy in History/Social Studies, Science, and Technical Subjects, 6–12. The CCSS do not prescribe instructional methodologies or rigid schedules of instruction. They only illustrate what a college- and career-ready high school senior should know and be able to do.

The CCSS depend on two critical soft skills: effective reading and effective writing. Though technically reading and writing happen mostly in English language arts classes, the CCSS weave effective reading and writing into every subject because success in college and the workplace depend on them (CCSS, p. 4). For reading, the CCSS focus on "text complexity" and strategies for students to increase their capacity to grapple with more difficult texts. For writing, the CCSS not only ask students to be aware of audience, task, and purpose, but also ask students to switch flawlessly between argumentative, informative, process, and narrative writing.

Another useful feature of the Common Core State Standards is that they are built on no more than ten College and Career Readiness (CCR) Anchor Standards for each content area. For example, in Reading, the ten CCRs are divided among four main concepts that are applied to all grades K–5: Key Ideas and Details, Craft and Structure, Integration of Knowledge and Ideas, and Range of Reading and Level of Complexity (p. 10). This limit of ten CCRs makes it easier for students, parents, and especially teachers to keep track of which standards have been mastered; ten is a manageable number (some states have 30 or 40 content standards that need to be mastered in the same discipline).

When I got to college, I know that I did not feel ready for it. I was lousy at managing my time for study between rigorous courses, demanding schedules, and keeping up with all of the assignments and due dates. Because I didn't know how to read or write critically, I felt like I was working real hard but not making much progress in some classes. I spent a lot of time memorizing vocabulary, formulas, and theories, but in some classes (linear algebra and analytic geometry) I never really understood how and why they fit together. Notice that my biggest concerns were not about acquiring specific content knowledge (although I was plenty worried about content too). The more intangible things that lead to success in college were the things I needed most. My content knowledge was weaker than I wanted, but I could not improve it without improving the soft skills first. These soft skills, like reading critically, are the things that I wish all of my teachers had taught me from kindergarten on up. That is the purpose of this book. I want to give educators like yourself, who deal with students of all ages, the insights, tools, and strategies to help you prepare your students to be successful using the college- and career-readiness measures of the Common Core State Standards.

In 2003, Dr. David Conley, then director of the Center for Education Policy Research at the University of Oregon, finished a three-year study on college-readiness standards entitled *Standards for Success*. This landmark document has become the cornerstone of many college-readiness programs worldwide, including the CCSS. The College Board has also adopted the information in this report and built on it by creating detailed college-readiness Standards for Success in each of its core disciplines for each middle- and high-school grade. In addition, the College Board designed a complete math and ELA curriculum called SpringBoard that takes the recommendations from the Standards for Success and back-maps them over the seven years of middle school and high school, assuring that they have been covered by the time the student graduates.

Rather than listing all the content knowledge and skills that need to be acquired and mastered before entering college, this book will focus on those oft-neglected soft skills that, almost uniformly, every college professor wishes that incoming freshman possessed.[1] Distilled out of the CCSS are ten distinct qualities for identifying college- and career-ready students that I have taken the liberty of labeling student traits. Students who are college- and career-ready are

1. Analytic Thinkers (they think about the parts and pieces of the whole)
2. Critical Thinkers (they think about effectiveness and validity)
3. Problem Solvers (this is more than a one size fits all heuristic)
4. Inquisitive (they have curiosity on steroids)
5. Opportunistic (they take advantage of learning opportunities—learn now rather than later)
6. Flexible (they are able and willing to cope with frustration and ambiguity)
7. Open Minded (they are willing to accept critical feedback)
8. Teachable (they are willing to adjust based on feedback)
9. Risk Takers (they are open to possible failure)
10. Expressive (they are able to communicate in writing and orally)

In this book, you will find a treasure trove of specific strategies that promote the growth and development of these college- and career-readiness traits. Each chapter will be composed of two parts: the "why" or theoretical part based on research, and the "how" part based on best practices.

I encourage you to read these chapters critically, or as Dr. Michael Schmoker, author of *Results Now* and *Focus*, suggests, "with pen in hand." Write all over the margins your doubts, questions, observations, and disagreements. Ultimately what you get out of this book is not what I have to say, but what you think about what I have to say, and that makes all the difference in what you learn from this book. Enjoy.

---

[1]In the Standards for Success study produced by Dr. Conley (2003), over 400 college and university professors were queried concerning the knowledge and skills necessary to be successful in their particular coursework.

Section I

Creating Thinkers

Introduction to Analytical Thinking,
Critical Thinking, and Problem Solving

 Analytical thinking and critical thinking are often lumped together with that other higher-order thinking skill (HOTS) called problem solving. In fact, in most literature, authors, researchers, and education gurus use analytical thinking, critical thinking, and problem solving as interchangeable terms that simply indicate "deeper" thinking. Part of the reason for the confusion is that these skills often appear to use some of the same thinking techniques. In actuality, however, what really occurs is that in order to think critically, the thinker must first think analytically. In order to problem solve, the thinker must think analytically and critically.

Let me clarify. Critical thinking and analytical thinking are not the same thing. To clarify the difference between these words, let's look at their etymology (study of word meaning). According to the dictionary, "analyze" means to break apart into essential elements. The opposite of analyze is synthesize, or put together. "Criticize" means to evaluate or make a judgment regarding the merits or faults. The opposite of criticize in one sense would be praise or in another sense, absence of judgment. Simply looking at the two definitions, it is obvious that two different skill sets are required. So why are they often lumped together? Perhaps we use the words as synonyms because they both require "hard" thinking or significant mental effort. Another reason may be that we just don't think it is important to distinguish between them, but to be honest with you, I feel we simply are suffering "a stupor of thought," or the absence of thinking.

To graphically illustrate the difference between analytical thinking and critical thinking, I have included Figure I.1, (drawn by my son Gideon Johnson, now a student at A&M). If you look at it carefully, you will see more than a series of Rubik's cubes placed in the form of a question mark. You will see that the cubes may appear to be random configurations of the cube except

Figure I.1 Rubik's Question (Gideon Johnson, 2012)

for the last one. In looking more closely, you will see that they are placed in a sequential pattern from most disorganized to most organized. Not only that, but if you pull out your own Rubik's cube and mimic the pattern, you will see something amazing. You will solve the riddle of the cube. That is pure analytical thinking at its best. There was no need for judgment when my son drew this image on the computer. OK, he did have to choose (be critical about) which design was best and what to include in the design, but showing how he solves the cube was pure analysis.

Benjamin Bloom (1956) made the specific distinction between analytical thinking (analysis) and critical thinking (evaluation), stating that the two skills differ in cognitive difficulty by two orders of magnitude (Lorin Anderson, in her revision of *Bloom's Taxonomy of the Cognitive Domain*, changed it so they only differ by one [Pohl, 2000]). So, according to Bloom, thinking critically is much more difficult than thinking analytically. The reason for this has already been discussed: in order to think critically, one must understand what one is criticizing. The way to understand something is to look at it analytically: break it down into parts, figure out how it works, classify it, etc. Once that is done, then critical thinking can be undertaken: asking why it works, looking for reasons, finding limits and exceptions, judging value, discovering errors, etc.

To clearly express the differences among these three thinking skills, I would like to share another example. Analytical thinking is what my son applied to the electric mixer to find out how it worked. He took it apart, piece-by-piece. He saw how the pieces fit together and how each part interacted with the other parts. With this analytic knowledge, he was able then to re-create the inner workings of the mixer on a computer drafting program and then send his drawings to a 3D printer to sculpt a plastic prototype. Now my son knows the intricate details of the mixer's inner workings, and he can apply that knowledge to the inner workings of other brands of mixers and other devices that use motors, cogs, and gears to rotate objects at high speeds, such as drills, fans, and remote-controlled cars.

Critical thinking (at least an order of magnitude more difficult according to Bloom) was employed when my son figured out why the mixer was not working (which is what had qualified the mixer for my son's learning experience in the first place). To discover why the mixer did not work required him to use the critical thinking skill of identifying the merits or faults of the mixer and its internal workings. He first determined the quality of the output of the mixer: the mixer made a lot of noise, but the beaters would not engage enough to mix the ingredients in the bowl. Then he identified the cause of the lack of motion of the beaters: the motor did not engage the beaters. Then he had to go back to analytical thinking to follow the chain of interactions from the beater to the motor until he discovered the faulty gear.

The final step would have been actually fixing the mixer, or solving the problem. My son then made a judgment (or did some more critical thinking) in order to determine if it was worth spending the time to fix the mixer or simply buy a new one. Since he knew the problem, he initially thought that he was going to fix it, and he had to employ some creativity to devise a plan or method to "fix" the problem. As it turned out, the plastic gears that spin the beaters had worn down to the point that they allowed the motor to run freely without engaging the beaters at all, which makes mixing by electric mixer more laborious than simply using a spoon (oh and that reminds me of the story of the fellow who bought a chainsaw . . . I digress[2]). My son, who is a diligent critical thinker, then determined *why* the gears were worn down. By reverting to analytical thinking again, he observed closely the problem area and discovered that when a plastic gear is used on a metal gear, the metal gear wins every time. He discovered a design flaw in the construction of the mixer. The first idea he thought of to solve the problem was to locate

---

[2]A backwoodsman went to a home improvement store and purchased a chainsaw to replace an old worn out saw. After a month, the backwoodsman returned the saw to the store. "It doesn't work worth a darn! I could hardly cut half the wood I normally do." The salesman, looking at the chainsaw and seeing nothing wrong, pulls the cord. The chainsaw starts easily with a roar. The backwoodsman jumps back. "Tarnation, what's all that racket? When I used it to saw, it was plumb silent!"

replacement parts for the damaged ones (the replacement parts, it turned out, were more expensive than the mixer), but since he knew that the problem was created by metal gears grinding down plastic ones, he surmised that this would be a temporary solution anyway. He thought he could fabricate new ones out of sturdier materials but realized he did not have the skills to create a die and smelt metal for new gear teeth, so that solution was rejected. Finally, he suggested we simply chuck the broken mixer and get a new one with metal gears. As you can see in this example, problem solving uses both analytical thinking and critical thinking along with creativity (creativity would be synthesis according to Bloom) to find the solutions.

The following three chapters discuss in detail analytical thinking, critical thinking, and problem solving as college- and career-readiness attributes. Each chapter describes the research and then provides strategies and techniques to help students acquire these attributes in order to be successful with the Common Core State Standards.

Analytical Thinkers

Analytical thinking: Thinking about the parts and pieces

Why Do Students Need to Be Analytical Thinkers?

Who was an analytical thinker? Hmm. Wasn't Aristotle the first to be classified as an analytic thinker? Aristotle, who lived from 384 to 322 B.C.E., was one of Plato's students. Later he tutored Alexander the Great. Aristotle took his place in Athens as a great educator in his own school, called the Lyceum. He was a keen observer, which is the first prerequisite of being analytical. After careful observations, he described the world he saw and broke it down into all of its pieces. In his writings, he describes his observations of multitudes of subjects. For example, he describes humans as having form and substance, and says that in order to be human, one must have both. This sounds pretty reasonable, but we know now that some of his observations were wrong. For example, his observations led him to believe that Earth was at the center of the universe and that all celestial objects revolved around it. This reminds me of the story by John Godfrey Saxe of blind men describing the elephant according to the parts they were touching. Each accurately described his own experience but entirely missed the target on what the whole elephant looked like.

Seymour Papert (1980), celebrated MIT professor, shared that his analytical thinking as a youth was greatly strengthened by the concept of gears, cogs, and wheels. Their interplay fascinated him, so he tried to figure out how moving one gear might affect the entire system and how all the gears and cogs changed speeds, torque, and directions. From his fascination with gears and cogs, Dr. Papert created a computer language to help students increase their analytical thinking by controlling the path of an electronic "turtle."

In the movie *I.Q.* (1994), the hero, Ed Walters, played by Tim Robbins, sailed through the first part of an "intelligence" test, which consisted of patterns of wooden blocks, complex interconnecting pieces, and a puzzle box. But he needed help from Albert Einstein, played by Walter Matthau, when it came to the actual "content" or principles of physics. As the story goes, Ed Walters was good at puzzles because he was an auto mechanic, accustomed to the intense analytical thinking involved with taking apart and putting back together transmissions.

Malcom Gladwell says that Bill Joy, the brilliant mind behind Unix, Java, and Sun Microsystems, is a success story because of the "10,000-hour rule"[3] and because he was born in the right place at the right time, which for the computer industry was 1953–1955. He is a computer programmer extraordinaire and an analytical thinker who can think in terms of procedures, heuristics, and algorithms. For him, coding computers is as easy as riding a bicycle. His analytical thinking includes two types of knowledge: he must know the capacity and operation of the computer and he must be fluent in the coding language that tells the computer what to do and how to do it.

All of those examples show what analytical thinking is and describe its limitations. Analytic thinkers are investigators, organizers, categorizers, labelers, and specifiers, but they only do these things within what they have experienced. For the most part, analysis is restricted to what can be seen or touched, manipulated or observed. Analytical thinkers use analytic strategies and analytic techniques to understand how things work, how they fit together, and how they relate to other things. Analytical thinkers use strategies such as logic to determine how things operate. Another strategy they use is to think in terms of systems and interactions among systems.

To support their chosen or preferred strategy, analytical thinkers use analytical thinking techniques such as SWOT, which identifies Strengths, Weaknesses, Opportunities and Threats; KWL (What Do I Know? What Do I Want to Know? What Did I Learn?); SQR4 (Survey, Question, Read, Recite, Rephrase, Review); or the now antiquated Whole Learning method (Title, Purpose, Resources, Activities, Consequences). We will be discussing these

---

[3]Malcolm Gladwell's book, *Outliers*, describes how people became successful. The 10,000-hour rule is what he discovered was the threshold of time that needed to be invested in practice for someone to become an expert or exceptional in their chosen venue. Gladwell illustrates this by explaining that great athletes, scientists, computer programmers, and even musicians (like the Beatles) reached this threshold, which allowed them to become superstars.

strategies and their supporting techniques for analytical thinking in the second half of this chapter.

Perhaps the best way to express the essence of analytic thinking is to use an example from one of the best thinkers around, Shel Silverstein. I love reading his poems because he takes common, self-evident statements, concepts, and household articles and turns them on their heads through his literal interpretations. Reading his work makes a person think, laugh, and then think some more. Using analytical thinking, Silverstein vividly recounts in verse the story of Melinda Mae who solved her whale problem one bite at a time. The heart of analytic thinking is taking a big task and breaking it down into bite-sized pieces, then looking at all the parts and making sense of them, one piece at a time. Sometimes it takes a bit of effort to find all the parts or identify that something is a unique part, but once the parts are all identified, then the thinker can figure them out. He can identify the purpose, methods, and interactions of each part until he knows how the whole thing works. This can be quite laborious if there are many parts. Vincent Ruggiero (2009) recounts the history of Walter Chrysler, who, as a railroad mechanic, purchased a Pierce Arrow automobile with the sole purpose of taking it apart, piece by piece, to discover how it worked and identify any possible ways to improve on it. We all know the rest of the story. Today we would call what he did reverse engineering, which is a common industrial practice, the movie *Paycheck* (2003) with Ben Affleck and Uma Thurman being a perfect futuristic example of this. Affleck plays Michael Jennings, the expert in reverse engineering who hires himself out to reverse an engineer competitor's technology. As a safeguard for the company, after the job is done, Jennings's memory of what he has just done is erased. The movie starts by giving an example of a holographic display that was reverse engineered. Jennings made it even better, discovering it did not even need the display in order to work. (So as to not leave you hanging if you haven't seen the movie, the plot shows Jennings in trouble after his last job and trying to figure out obscure clues of the future that he left for himself. It's a good movie.)

The Importance of Analytic Strategies and Techniques

Jigsaw puzzles are full of pieces, which require us to think analytically in order to assemble them. We have all tried to solve jigsaw puzzles and have our own preferred methods. I think everyone would agree that the hardest way to solve a jigsaw puzzle is to try to connect one piece to another piece by simply testing each piece until you find the one that fits (this is what a computer would do—called a Boolean search). This strategy might work on a junior puzzle with ten pieces, but it would take years to complete a puzzle with a thousand pieces. Good jigsaw puzzlers use a strategy to guide their actions and techniques. They have a mindset for looking at the solution to the whole problem. By adhering to this mindset, they can finish the puzzle in the shortest amount of time. For example, some puzzlers focus more on the colors rather than the shapes of the pieces, while other puzzlers focus on the big picture and form of the entire puzzle.

I have heard of another strategy that depends solely on the form of the pieces. You assemble the jigsaw puzzle upside down and depend purely on the shape of the pieces. It is plausible that the colors and images might be, and in the most difficult puzzles are, designed to mislead and confuse the puzzler.

The jigsaw examples demonstrate that good analytical thinkers always have a guiding strategy and several supporting techniques at their beck and call to help them increase understanding and make the right connections, jigsaw-like.

Analytical Thinking and the Common Core

Analytic thinkers are philosophers, college professors, transmission mechanics, and computer programmers. They reverse engineer, tinker, and solve puzzles by using strategies to guide their thinking and employing techniques as if they were tools. The CCSS require that students not only acquire the necessary knowledge but also use analytical thinking in order to gain that knowledge. This means that students must be proficient at reading, analyzing (breaking apart), ". . . and enjoying complex works of literature" (Common Core State Standards Initiative [CCSSI], 2010a, p. 3) of all genres, mediums, and methods. Students must identify underlying structures, thoughts, and motives. Piecing together the puzzles is only the means to gain understanding, but it is an entirely necessary process in order for learners to make sense of the world in ways that make sense to them, right or wrong.

The role of the teacher is to show students analytical thinking strategies and techniques and then create learning opportunities that require students to use them in order to learn content and gain abilities. The CCSS identify overarching College and Career Readiness (CCR) Anchor Standards for each content area that guide teachers in selecting strategies for knowledge and skills acquisition in mathematics, English language arts, and literacy. For Reading, CCR Standard 10 establishes the grade-level progression of text complexity that students should master as they gain skills in analytic reading (and critical reading). The magic of reading is that through the words of others, students don't have to travel to England to learn the deductive skills of Agatha Christie's Hercule Poirot. Through analytic reading, students can travel back in time and look over the shoulders of John Jay, James Madison, and Alexander Hamilton as they write the federalist papers, or Shakespeare as he pens the poignant messages of *The Tempest*. Through analytic reading, students can envision the future, get into the brain of Albert Einstein, and really understand gravity through the General Theory of Relativity.

The second part of this chapter will help you to learn about effective, best-practice analytical thinking strategies and supporting techniques for each strategy that you can immediately apply in your classroom.

How to Help Students Become Analytical Thinkers

Analytical thinking is the backbone of all learning. Unfortunately, well-meaning teachers and professors, much like the proverbial tinkerer with the alarm clock, often take a subject and break it down analytically, but forget to put it back together, which makes it essentially useless for the sleeper and the students. In this half of the chapter, you will read about ways to help students take ideas and concepts apart and then reassemble them (Mindedge, 2010).

S T R A T E G Y

Abstract Thinking to Enhance Analytical Thinking

Give teenagers the old piece of wisdom, "A rolling stone, gathers no moss." Typical teenage response: "Mick Jagger has moss?" Tell teenagers, "Don't cry over spilt milk." They'll say, "It's only milk, why cry?" Say, "Too many cooks spoil the soup." They'll respond, "I hate soup." Mention "water under the bridge." They'll say, "Of course there is water under a bridge!" Say, "A tiger's stripes do not change." You'll hear "Duh." Tell teenagers, "Birds of a feather, flock together." "Yeah, those grackles downtown are so annoying." There must be millions of them.

A college-ready student can think figuratively or, in other words, can associate abstract ideas with concrete examples. One of the best ways to help students think abstractly is to engage them in the ancient wisdom of metaphors and adages. While not exactly parallel, thinking figuratively through metaphors, analogies, and allusions is a first step toward thinking abstractly. Initially, students' reactions will be like the ones above, but with a little practice, they will be able to arrive at the real meaning of the sayings. Thinking abstractly is useful for understanding the richness of both classic and modern literature. Carroll's *Alice's Adventures in Wonderland*, Dr. Seuss's *Horton Hears a Who*, and Milton's *Paradise Lost* would be incomprehensible without the ability to think abstractly.

The reason that algebra, geometry, and general mathematics challenge students is that they require students to think abstractly. The bane of most students—solving word problems—involves transforming something concrete into abstract symbols and numbers. Most problem-solving techniques require students to step back (figuratively) from the problem at hand (it could be at foot) and state the problem in abstract terms.

In order to help my students improve their abstract thinking and their skill in using the Spanish language, I printed a "dicho" (a saying) on the board, such as my favorite one, "*En boca cerrada no entra mosca!*" (In a closed mouth, flies don't enter). I asked students to decipher the Spanish and then provide the real meaning. Once we got past the literal interpretations, students were usually able to arrive at approximate meanings. Some *dichos* stumped them at first: "*Al hambriento, no hay pan duro*" (To the hungry, there is no hard bread) or "*En casa del herrero, cuchillo de palo*" (In the house of the blacksmith, a wooden knife).

I found that the key to helping them the most was counterintuitive. Part of me wanted to just give them the answer, but in terms of actual learning, the best course of action was *not* to give the students the answer, but to let them figure it out and only nudge them a bit if they got stuck. So I put on my Socratic robes and asked questions. Trying to answer my Socratic questions was very hard for my students in the beginning, but with practice, they got it. They began to see the deeper messages in the *dichos* and were able to transfer that skill to see deeper messages in Spanish humor and literature. It was always illuminating and inspiring to watch as students caught the joke, or the meaning of a passage of literature. Students are smarter than we give them credit for sometimes—*El león no es como lo pintan* (the lion is not how it is painted).

S T R A T E G Y

Socratic Questioning

Bite your tongue and quit telling students what they should think. Making *them* come up with something is probably the first strategy that should guide our teaching. We do them no favors by just giving them the answers, especially when they don't even ask for them. Students remember the answers they come up with themselves and feel more satisfaction.

TECHNIQUE: *Answer a question with a question.* When a student asks a question, the teacher has a variety of questions that can be asked back to help the student: Questions that seek clarification, questions that probe assumptions, questions that ask for reasons and evidence. For example, an elementary teacher may ask questions like the following:

- ♦ Questions that seek clarification: What do you mean by saying the sunfish looks like a pancake?
- ♦ Questions that probe assumptions: What does the shape of the sunfish have to do with its name?
- ♦ Questions that ask for reasons and evidence: Why doesn't the sunfish look like other fishes?

S T R A T E G Y

Whole Part Whole

The whole part whole strategy, or as some call it, the hamburger approach to learning, is a way of organizing learning activities so that students end with the whole, rather than just associated parts. It requires presenting students with the whole problem, then looking at that problem using analytical tools to discover the parts, and then when all the parts are identified and understood, putting the hamburger back together with some sort of application or evaluation of learning that requires integrated solutions. For example, "What is the math problem trying to accomplish? Can you identify the error in the calculation of this problem? Great! Now fix the error and see if the goal of the problem was reached."

TECHNIQUE: If—then and What if . . . Asking the questions, "If this happens, then what will the result be?" and "What if this happens, how will this change that?" is a technique that helps student understand the interconnectedness of the whole. When students start messing with the parts, there will be consequences to other parts and to the whole. Students must think analytically in order to identify the consequences and predict the outcomes. The concept of systems thinking will also help students understand that there are different outcomes for systems. Systems can be static or they can seek balance. There are growth systems and systems of decline. Dependent systems, interdependent systems, and independent systems can be described by dominoes lined up. A dependent system is one in which the dominos cannot fall unless struck by another system of dominoes. An interdependent system is similar. Not only can one domino from another system begin the cascade, but one of its own dominoes can trigger other cascades in the other system. An independent system cannot be triggered by another domino but may be able to trigger other systems' dominoes.

TECHNIQUE: Finish the story. One project I did as the gifted and talented director of a small school district was student walking tours of historical San Antonio. After the tours, students were asked to identify one element of the tour and eliminate it from San Antonio history. Then they were asked to postulate on the ripple effects that that one historical instance would or could have had on modern San Antonio, the nation, and the world. One of the sites on the tour was the Alamo. One of the groups postulated that if the Battle of the Alamo had not occurred, then Texas would have been a part of Mexico at the time of the Civil War, and therefore the large amounts of cattle that supplied the confederate troops may not have been available. This would have altered the course of the war as well as its aftermath.

S T R A T E G Y

Logic

Analytical thinking assumes there are reasons and underlying rules that govern the way things are and the way things work. Knowing the rules is half the battle. Being able to correctly apply the rules is the other half. Helping students identify and utilize the governing rules is a way to organize their thinking in a logical fashion.

TECHNIQUE: *Syllogisms.* Syllogisms are tri-part logical statements that help students analyze conclusions using deductive and inductive methods (there really is no difference between deductive and inductive thinking—they both look at facts and make a guess at the meaning or the conclusion based on those facts). The classic syllogism is "Animals have four legs; a dog has four legs; therefore a dog is an animal." Switching things around a bit by using quantifying terminology to refine the relationships—*such as, all, some, none, always,* etc.—is an easy way to enhance that syllogism and get students to think deeper.

TECHNIQUE: *Logical operations, AND, If, Or, NOT Or.* Most people do not realize that they use logical operations all the time. A simple Boolean search on Google is a lesson on logical operators. Students can search for (appropriate) topics and see the difference in the results returned by adding AND or NOT Or. Applying these same logical operations to the analysis of text can help students identify the main theme(s) from the text and check the sequencing or logical flow of the argument. Geometric proofs follow logical operations, as do algebraic theories and postulates. In reading Shakespeare, students can map the concepts with AND, Or, and NOT Or to understand what is really being stated.

TECHNIQUE: *Program a partner.* Have one partner create movement actions for the other partner to follow, much like the Logo Mindstorms' turtle.[4] This requires that both the designer and the follower think

---

[4]Seymour Paper, the MIT professor who wrote the book *Mindstorms*, created a computer programming language for children that he called "Logo." This language allowed children to control a small robot with a pen that could be raised or lowered. The robot sort of looked like a turtle, so that is what he called it. The language allowed children to give the turtle directions (right, left, forward, etc.) and distances.

analytically of distance, direction, and speed. And it requires that both students agree on the units of measure for distance, speed, and direction. If the technology is available, Lego robotics are perfect tools to teach logic. For older students, blindfolding the follower forces both students to think about navigating the classroom full of obstacles and the importance of being precise in giving instructions. I had my Spanish One students do this to learn the commands for giving directions in Spanish.

STRATEGY

Identifying Differences and Similarities

In the seminal book *Classroom Instruction That Works*, Marzano et al. (2001) identify that the classroom strategy with the highest effect-size (positive results) based on their meta research was identifying differences and similarities. They are careful to explain that although simply telling students the differences and similarities is a powerful tool, student-directed methods are also powerful. Always keep in mind that learning transfers from one concept to the concept that is being learned if the student is able to recognize similarities or differences in both. Being able to ride a bike transfers to being able to ride a motorcycle. Though the experience is fundamentally different, the basic skills necessary are nearly identical. The gifted educator will make connections to prior knowledge and stack the deck, so to speak, to make it easy for students to analyze the similarities and differences for themselves.

TECHNIQUE: *Methods of classification—genus, phylum, species.*
My daughter loved the game of twenty-one questions, and for Christmas one year, we gave her a computerized version. It consists of a plastic ball that fits in your hand and that plays the game with you by asking you to respond yes or no to a series of questions printed on a small, liquid-crystal screen. Amazingly, every time I played with it, this little device always arrived at the thing that I had chosen. I had to work hard to guess something that it would not figure out. It is almost spooky . . . unless you understand the principle behind the game. Experts at twenty-one questions (usually eight to twelve years old) will tell you that the way to win the game is to refine the

target sample with questions that classify the object as part of a genus, then a phylum, and then a species. Once it is at that level, it is simple to identify the species. There are multitudes of ways to help students categorize, including grouping charts and tables, mind maps, and Venn diagrams. Of particular usefulness is computer software that helps students easily connect the dots. This software includes the Microsoft Office Suite, Freemind, Inspiration, Prezi, and HyperStudio. In Excel and Word, students can create tables, graphs, and charts showing categories and similarities and differences. In PowerPoint, students can present and describe their discoveries of similarities or differences. Freemind and Inspiration are programs that help students intuitively organize information in mind maps, flowcharts, and outlines. Prezi is an intriguing presentation tool that allows students to present their topics at the macro level and describe similarities and differences by literally drilling down, magnifying the picture to reveal the connections. HyperStudio is a rich, open-ended multimedia presentation/creation tool that uses stacks to contain content. As the name suggests, hyper connections are made among the stacks to allow students to create complex interconnections that do not have to be sequential, as in PowerPoint.

TECHNIQUE: Identifying patterns—textual CSI. As already discussed, jigsaw puzzles are fun because we have to identify patterns that match. Finding the next piece to a pattern is a mainstay of intelligence tests and cognition exercises. In the classroom, patterns can be found in the styles of different writing genres. Present students with several different genres of text and have them analyze the technical, connotative, or figurative interpretations of words and phrases in each. Students will then analyze the structure of the sentences and paragraphs. Finally, students will identify the points of view and the intended audience of the text (College and Career Readiness Anchor Standards for Reading 4, 5, and 6). The task for students will be to identify the genre[5] of the text according to purpose: narrative: sequence of events; procedural: how to; expository: explanation; hortatory (persuasive): get someone to do something; and descriptive: list characteristics. Then students can identify the text type.[6] Perhaps the

---

[5] *Genre* is one of those words that changes meaning according to whom you are speaking. In literature, this is particularly true because the word is used so often in so many different contexts. For an interesting exploration into its meaning, read David Lee's research, "Genres, registers, text types, domains and styles: Clarifying the concepts and navigating the path through the BNC Jungle" (retrieved March 22nd, 2012 from http://llt.msu.edu/vol5num3/pdf/lee.pdf). For all intents and purposes, and in this document, *genre* means "category."

[6] For a no-frills selection of ideas for concept-mapping types of texts, se the following site, retrieved March 22, 2012: www.cheney268.com/learning/organizers/TypesText.htm

easiest text type to identify because of its obvious patterns is poetry. The five-paragraph essay follows a different pattern than the newspaper article, which follows a different pattern than the one used by an epitaph.

TECHNIQUE: *Frames for writing.* Marzano et al. (2001), in *Classroom Instruction That Works*, identify a writing technique used to analyze certain genres and types of literature (pp. 35–42). The authors share multiple types of frames that students can use to analyze corresponding literature. Marzano includes a frame for narratives, a frame for expository writing called the "Topic-Restriction-Illustration" frame, a definitions frame, an argumentation frame, a problem/solution frame, and a conversation frame. The frames serve as guides and templates for students to systematically identify the structure and characteristics of certain texts.

TECHNIQUE: *What's not the same.* Discovering what is wrong or odd with the problem could include determining the differences, which is the odd man out, or which element doesn't belong ("One of these things is not like the other, one of these things just doesn't belong . . ." —remember *Sesame Street*?) This technique is enhanced when the pattern is clearly identified, because what doesn't fit the pattern will seem to shine as if written in neon lights. In addition, after reading a selection, once the title, purpose, resources, activities, and consequences have been identified, a valid analytical question is, "What's missing?" Many times additional meaning can be derived as much by what is *not* stated as by what is.

TECHNIQUE: *SWOT.* Using a process to identify patterns such as SWOT, which identifies strengths, weaknesses, opportunities, and threats, can help students lay the foundation for making decisions (evaluation in Bloom's Taxonomy) regarding possible courses of action and solutions. (See Figure 1.1.) This technique is an expansion of the effective pro and con process used to organize thinking for persuasive (hortatory) writing. Not only do you utilize the pros (strengths) and cons (weaknesses), but the results of the choices are considered separately in opportunities and threats. An interesting analysis technique is to juxtapose these opposites in a table and force the analysis of the situation's possibilities concurrently. Lively discussion can ensue to determine which of the items belong to both strengths and opportunities, opportunities and weaknesses, threats and strengths, and threats and weaknesses.

TECHNIQUE: *KWL* (What do I know? What do I want to know? What did I learn?). KWL and its many variations were designed and are most

Figure 1.1 SWOT

	Strength	Weakness
Opportunity		
Threat		

powerful as prereading strategies to help students prepare for reading by anticipating information that might be in the reading selection. Students do this by looking at clues such as pictures on the book's cover, the book's title and author, the table of contents, the back of the book, the introductory paragraph, etc. (Szabo, 2006). Then students must ask themselves, What do I know (about what I am going to read)? This first question has misled many teachers to use KWL as a pretesting method for different subjects because this first question is the basis of any pretest—to find out what students know before teaching begins. However, I must clarify that this question is focused solely on the information gathered from looking at the cover of the book, flipping a few pages, interpreting the title, and knowing something about the author. The student will do some deductive thinking, again based on the perusal of the outside of the book, to guess what the book is about. Based on what they have just gleaned from the cover of the book or skimming the article, the students then ask themselves, "What do I want to know? (or in other words, what has piqued my interest, or what am I curious to find out, or how has the author of this text invited me to know more?)" Students should answer this question not merely as matter of preference, but as a form of inquiry—"Why did the author write this book?" and "What am I to learn from it?" Some teachers are tempted to also misuse this step and make the false assumption that students want to know about radioactive isotopes, the vertices of a triangle, or the date of the battle of 1812. Finally, after reading the selection, students write what was learned from the reading. KWL has been applied with various degrees of success as a pretesting procedure in many subjects, but as I've explained, it is most effective as a prereading strategy.

TECHNIQUE: SQR4 (Survey, Question, Read, Recite, Rephrase, Review [Meyer & Kelley, 2007]). Similar to KWL, the SQR4 reading strategy and its variations can help students understand what they read because it is an analytical process that is ingrained into the students. It is intended for students to do the SQR4 automatically so that as they read, they go through the six steps. **Survey** simply means to scan the document, look at the headings, pay attention to the titles, and get a feel for where the document is going with the topic. **Question** refers to the act of rephrasing the subject headings as questions so that when they **Read**, they are looking for the answers to those questions. **Reciting** can be done while reading paragraphs at a time (most effective), or after they have finished a section. It means what it says—students use their mouths and say what they learned from what they read—i.e., the answers to the questions they just posed. **Rephrase** is another way of saying summarize, and **Review** means that they look at all the notes they made while they were reading. There are several variations of this technique, but they all follow the same idea that for students to get the most out of what they read, they must they think analytically about what they read, take notes, and review those notes. Those steps are essential for improving understanding (and recall).

TECHNIQUE: Sequencing. When students are asked to write process papers about how to solve a math problem, they must use analytical thinking to determine the best sequence of events. The steps and associated explanations must follow a logical order and be replicable. However in real life, many times we do not get to create a "how to do" process; instead, we come upon a scene and have to determine, "what was done?" To help students acquire this technique, a teacher can have students tell stories about photographs cut from magazines. The need for logical sequencing is developed by providing students with a final ending picture and a mix of photos of a situation, and requesting that students place the pictures in a logical order to explain what happened. A similar exercise can be done with writing. Certain stylistic elements of an essay or a narrative provide clues as to the possible sequential order. The introduction and body of a persuasive essay telegraph what comes next, while the conclusion indicates what has been discussed prior. Simply jumble the paragraphs and have students decide the logical sequence of the paragraphs. This forces students to compare, contrast, and categorize each paragraph in terms of relative importance. For interest's sake, a news article could be analyzed, recognizing that the format is entirely different; in the first paragraph are the important details, and each succeeding paragraph is either chronological or ordered by relative importance.

TECHNIQUE: Reverse engineering. Similar to the reverse process paper, reverse engineering is a valuable technique for helping students identify similarities and differences. I participated with a group of ninth graders as they were given an assignment to reverse engineer a situation in a Ford PAS class. Ford PAS stands for Partnerships for Advanced Studies and is a STEM/Business inquiry-based program, sponsored by the Ford Fund (not the Ford Foundation—different pockets of money, same company). I observed these ninth graders reverse engineer the breaking of a clay pot with a hammer. Based on the location of the pieces on the ground after the breaking incident and the size of the pieces scattered about, the students were able to re-create the hammer's exact location of impact on the clay pot, as well as the force and angle of the impact. In order to do this, the students had to find all the pieces, graph their relative locations, use the pieces to reassemble the pot (Super Glue works best), mark the impact point on the reassembled pot, and then analyze the dispersion graph to determine angle and force of the blow. Reverse engineering can be applied to more than clay pots and computers (have you seen the movie *Paycheck* (2003) by Ben Affleck?). Reverse engineering principles can be applied to all sorts of math problems: given a solution, determine how it was derived; chemistry problems: given a solution, determine the process to create the solution; history problems: given the gross national product, determine the economic factors that caused it; and English problems: given a Sherlock Holmes solution, determine the deductive path he used to solve the case.

Metacognitive Modeling

Analytic thinking, like any muscle, improves with practice. It is essential that students not only learn to *use* analytical thinking but also *become* analytical thinkers. The reason students struggle in school, especially in math and science, can be traced directly to their lack of ability to think analytically. When teachers use metacognitive modeling to show students how to think analytically, create daily learning experiences in which analytical strategies are required, take time to show students how to use multiple analytical thinking techniques, and then let students apply those skills, they are preparing their students to be successful in college or university studies and careers.

Finally, analytical thinking is incredibly important for students to master because five of the ten CCSS College and Career Readiness Anchor Standards for K–5 Reading use analytical thinking:

2. Determine central ideas or themes of a text and **analyze** their development; summarize the key supporting details and ideas.

3. **Analyze** how and why individuals, events, and ideas develop and interact over the course of a text.

4. Interpret words and phrases as they are used in a text, including determining technical, connotative, and figurative meanings, and **analyze** how specific word choices shape meaning or tone.

5. **Analyze** the structure of texts, including how specific sentences, paragraphs, and larger portions of the text (e.g., a section, chapter, scene, or stanza) relate to each other and the whole.

9. **Analyze** how two or more texts address similar themes or topics in order to build knowledge or to compare the approaches the authors take. (bold added; CCSS, p.10)

Chapter 2

Critical Thinkers

Critical thinking: Thinking about effectiveness and validity

Why Do Students Need to Be Critical Thinkers?

Maybe I have watched too many movies and am paranoid, but I believe that people and especially students are far too trusting. "Trust no one!" the hero or heroine is always told, and it turns out that the person who said not to trust anyone is the one who should not have been trusted. What we hear at schools is a different matter altogether. Students are expected to trust the teacher and the textbook. The system is designed for knowledge to trickle down from those who know to those who do not know. That knowledge is implicitly assumed to be correct, especially by the younger students. No teacher will argue with you, however, that more and more often, students are willing to challenge the teacher (mostly their authority and sometimes their knowledge). It takes a lot of confidence for students to challenge a teacher, and it takes a self-confident teacher to be able to handle these challenges in positive ways. But isn't that what we want? Isn't that what industry wants? Isn't that what colleges and universities want?

What I mean is that we want students to think critically (evaluate the merits and faults) of what they are learning and not accept blindly what the teacher or textbook says. Teachers have an obligation to prepare students to be successful in the Common Core State Standards. Reading and writing critically are constant literacy themes that permeate the CCSS. In fact, the CCSS for English Language Arts state of the students who meet the Standards, "They habitually perform the critical reading necessary to pick carefully through the staggering amount of information available today in print and digitally" (p. 3).

Parents should be asking teachers, "Are my children being prepared to be critical thinkers so that when they get to college, they can stand on their own?" More importantly, parents should be asking, "Does my child know how to be a critical thinker in order to be an effective learner?" Sure, critical thinking is all about doubting what you read, hear, or see and asking the hard questions, the politically-charged questions, and the socially inconvenient questions. But how does that help students learn better? Both parts of this chapter, the Why and the How, will strive to answer that question.

Teachers' Perspectives of Critical Thinking

In this chapter, and frankly in all of the chapters of this book, I want to center our "thinking" around what you might consider to be a selfish concept for teachers, considering all the emphasis on student learning: "How does critical thinking help me, the teacher, in the classroom?" To begin this conversation, let's look at the pros and cons of critical thinking (see Figure 2.1). Just like a rose has its thorns, so does critical thinking. In the "pro" column are the things that make critical thinking enjoyable and profitable for students. In the "con" column are the typically unmentioned side effects of critical thinking (similar to a warning label on medicinal cures, written in impossibly small type). I am not sure, nor do I believe, that the pro and con sides can be weighted equally as if in a balance. So in the table, no particular priority or order was imposed to make the list. However, in my opinion, the benefits described in the "pro" column far outweigh the irritating side-effects of the "con" column. If I figuratively crush all of the items in the "pro" column into a single crucible of thought and grind it up real good, what emerges in the uniform powder is the unique and powerful idea, "Critical thinking helps students be more efficient learners."

The idea that critical thinking makes students more effective learners sounds pretty obvious, doesn't it? ("Duh!" some would say.) Common sense dictates that the more we get students to think critically, the better they become at it. Basic, right? Perhaps, but do you know why it works that way, what benefits there are for a teacher, and how teachers can easily bring critical thinking into their lessons? We will look at the "how" in the other half of this chapter, but let's tackle the first two questions now. The answers have to do with the brain and how it works.

One of my favorite authors has some pretty outlandish things to say about thinking and the brain. Dr. Daniel Willingham (2010), a noted cognitive psychologist, wrote a book that I think every teacher should read and then give to every parent to read. It is appropriately called *Why Students Don't Like School*.

Figure 2.1 How Does Critical Thinking Help Me as a Classroom Teacher?

Critical Thinking Pro	Critical Thinking Con
It makes learning more enjoyable and palatable for the learner.	It is not quick.
It makes learning memories permanent.	It is frustrating.
It makes learning deeper.	It is overwhelming.
It makes learning naturally more connected.	Nothing is believable.
It makes independent thinkers.	It challenges prior knowledge and assumptions.
It increases content and concept understanding.	It doesn't rest or stop; it is hard to turn off.
It inspires and fuels additional learning.	It can be wrong or faulty.
It establishes learner confidence.	It can be misused.
It satisfies a basic human need to make sense of the world.	It is voracious.
It prepares students for college.	It ruins fantasy.
It honors the efforts students and parents make to come to school.	It does not respect authority or friendship.
It fosters self-confidence.	It promotes argument and debate.
It develops habits of mind.	It develops habits of mind.

Dr. Willingham, right off the bat, tells his readers that they stink at thinking. Or was it think at stinking? Anyway, he says that humans are not good at thinking and so for this reason we have an enormous brain between our ears that helps us find all sorts of ways to avoid thinking. We use routines and habits instead of thinking to get by in everything we do. Habits are formed from memory, not thinking, and we are nothing if not habit-forming creatures. Try going to bed without brushing your teeth, or putting the left sock on first, or folding your arms a different way . . . you get the idea. We are full of habits—some good, some bad, and some indifferent. Most of what we do is from memory, not from thinking. Once in a while, we run across something new and have to think, but more often than not, we think only long enough to remember something similar, and then we don't have to think anymore. That is why experiencing new things is so exhausting—it forces us to think more than we are used to.

Dr. Willingham is a sly one though. He brings up an interesting conundrum. Humans are horrible thinkers, but as it turns out, we *like* thinking. Go figure. On one hand, we hate habits and boring routine, but we are awesome at making them, and on the other hand, we are terrible at thinking, but we enjoy it. We get a kick out of being stumped and having to figure something out. We love to solve problems, especially other people's problems. We are addicted to puzzles . . . up to a point. If the puzzle is too hard, it becomes a downer instead of an upper (is that too eighties-ish?). In other words, we love to be challenged just a bit over our capacity, but if the challenge is too hard, we become frustrated and angry, and the hormone cortisol is released, causing our hippocampuses to stop all thought, and we become human vegetables! Or . . . we simply disengage and do something else.

So why am I telling you all of this, you wonder? I'm getting to a very important point, although I have made a few already—students' brains are designed to depend on memory so they don't have to think; students like thinking, but we can't and shouldn't assume students are good at thinking because they are not (neither are we); and don't make the critical thinking too hard or students will give up. The point I really want to make is that savvy teachers can use their creative skills to design learning activities that give students the opportunity to try critical thinking, push students to the point their brains begins to hurt, and then—quick—give students a test before they forget it. No, no, no—let me finish that last sentence differently. And then ask students to create something with their newfound knowledge to show they really know it. Yes, that is much better!

If you recall, the point of this conversation was to demonstrate that critical thinking makes students more efficient learners. Ok, so now we have arrived at the pinnacle point in the explanation of critical thinking. What Dr. Willingham suggests is that when teachers get students to think, they stimulate memory. And I quote, "Memory is the residue of thought" (p. 41). After doing all of that hard thinking, what is left over? Memory! So why is that a selfish idea? Because—drum roll please—if students can remember something, we don't have to teach it again! We are done, finished, terminados! We can go on to something else. Everybody is happy! Yahoo!

If such a happy ending were easy to achieve, then every teacher would be doing it, right? Some teachers are doing it—students are learning at incredible rates in their classes. But more of us need to be doing it. Critical thinking in classrooms does not usually happen by chance. I should say, productive critical thinking does not happen by chance. It doesn't happen at all without a careful teacher setting the groundwork for it. How do I know that? Think about it. Students are always thinking critically, especially about each other, about cafeteria food, about school in general, and of course, about you. You might call it complaining. Benjamin Bloom would call it evaluating—the hardest cognitive activity to perform. I heard of a teacher who received a devastatingly honest e-mail from a student describing what the teacher was not doing in the classroom, but should be doing, including what specific things the teacher could be doing to fix the problems in the classroom. All this came from a sixth grader! Students know good teaching from bad teaching, but most of the time are too polite (or intimidated) to say anything. The good part of this story is that the teacher, rather than getting all upset—well, after getting all upset—took the message to heart and is now focusing on student learning, getting organized, and dealing with unruly students by channeling their energy into more useful learning activities. But that is another book entirely.

I once walked into a history class with the principal in tow and observed that all the desks were lined up in straight rows and students were at various stages of inattention, ostensibly answering the questions at the end of a chapter. The teacher was not expecting us because this was a surprise walk-through observation. As soon as we walked in, the teacher, who was sitting behind his desk doing something with the computer, stood up, faced the class, and asked a great higher-order thinking question. Observing the puzzled looks of the students, the teacher restated the question . . . with still no response. Changing tactics, the teacher asked a series of questions calculated to guide students to the answer he was seeking. A few light bulbs went on as some students caught the drift of what the teacher was trying to do, but students were still floundering, unable to answer correctly the teacher's simpler questions. The teacher persisted, asking probing question after probing question, to no avail. The principal and I left the classroom. As we walked down the corridor, I turned to the principal and asked, "What did you see?"

He responded, "The teacher knows how to ask good questions, but the students don't know how to answer them."

"Why couldn't the students answer the questions?" I probed.

The principal looked at me quizzically and replied, "I don't understand it. He is one of our best teachers. Students from his class always score well on state tests."

"It doesn't appear that the students knew the answers," the principal continued, "and it is obvious that they were not accustomed to answering critical thinking questions."

"So students need to know something in order to answer critical thinking questions," I stated. "And students need practice at answering them," I surmised, while the principal nodded agreement.

The moral of this story is that just like this history teacher's experience, it would be a waste of time for a teacher to start asking deep critical thinking questions if the students have little content knowledge, and the corollary moral is that for students to be able to answer critical thinking questions, they need to know how to think critically.

Critical Thinking in the Common Core

The CCSS for English language arts, social studies, science, technical subjects, and math require students to think critically. Figure 2.2 indicates which of the CCSS CCR Anchor Standards require critical thinking.

Figure 2.2 Critical Thinking Required by the Common Core State Standards

	1	2	3	4	5	6	7	8	9	10
K–5 Reading	✔					✔	✔	✔		
K–5 Writing							✔	✔	✔	
K–5 Speaking and Listening		✔	✔	✔						
K–5 Language			✔	✔						
6–12 Reading	✔			✔		✔	✔	✔		
6–12 Writing	✔						✔	✔	✔	
6–12 Speaking and Listening		✔	✔	✔						
6–12 Language			✔	✔						
6–12 Literacy in History/SS, Science, and Technical Subjects										
Reading	✔			✔		✔	✔	✔		
Writing	✔						✔	✔	✔	
Mathematical Practices	✔		✔					✔		

How to Help Students Think Critically

S T R A T E G Y

Helping Students Read Critically

Thomas asks, "How do you know that?"
Susan responds, "It says so right here in the textbook."
Thomas counters, "How does the textbook know that?"
Susan shrugs her shoulders, ". . . ?"
We have a generation of students who do not know how to read things with a grain of salt (most likely they would wonder what salt

had to do with reading). They are trained to automatically trust the textbook or, for that matter, to trust anything that is written.

How do we go about fixing this? First of all, we have to get students to read and then get them to read critically. Mem Fox, in her book *Reading Magic* (2001), states that the love of reading has to start young. Parents and teachers have to read at least 1,000 books to children to prepare them to read on their own (p. 17). She also states that if you want your child to stay at home and be close to family, "do not read them stories about the Amazon rain forests." As it turned out, she made the mistake of reading books about France to her young daughter, which prompted her daughter to want to read (know) more about France as she grew older. And guess where her daughter lived when she was twenty, having the time of her life in a new career (p. 128)? Dr. Schmoker, in his book *Results Now* (2006), recounts how reading helped Mike Rose transform himself from an educationally uninterested, nearly illiterate student to that of a successful college professor. Rose went to school in Los Angeles. Until tenth grade, he only went through the motions of learning in school. With his poor literacy, going to school made him feel embarrassed rather than challenged. His tenth grade teacher finally changed all that by exposing Rose and the other students to a heavy dose of challenging literature, by having students talk about what they read, and by having students write about the issues in the books. Today, Mike Rose is a full professor at UCLA's Graduate School of Education and Information Studies. Schmoker states emphatically that "Generous amounts of close, purposeful reading, rereading, writing, and talking, as underemphasized as they are in K–12 education, are the essence of authentic literacy" (2006, p. 53).

Reading has to be synonymous with thinking. How can you have the one without the other? Reading is an active learning method, as opposed to listening, which is passive. In order to read, students must be physically engaged—their eye movement tracks words, they turn the pages (or click the mouse or flick the page), they mentally decode symbols to sounds to meaning, they carry a storyline or topic flow in short-term memory, and they arrive at understanding through assimilation of mental images produced by reading the words. With all of that creative learning juice flowing in students' brains while they read, it would be a shame to not take advantage of it. Schmoker shares a simple, helpful strategy: "Read with a pen in hand." As students read, they should make notes in the margins, underline, circle, and highlight. What? Write in the book? I remember purchasing used books for college that were already highlighted and had notes in them, and they actually helped me study. Didn't they help you? So what is the shelf life of a typical school textbook? Five years? During those five years, do we want the only things written in the textbooks to be graffiti or profanity? Not going to budge? Well, if students can't write in their books, at least they can take notes on a separate piece of paper about what they read.

We should teach students to identify concepts while they read and then judge which one is a key concept. Authors tend to do that for students anyway by providing topic headings and subheadings. Then teachers need to help students identify kernels of evidence supporting the key concepts. Using Cornell Notes is a perfect way to do this. Let me be perfectly clear here. Cornell Notes, done right, is NOT just a note-taking tool—it is an enhanced thinking process. Do you recall what the residue of thinking is according to Dr. Daniel Willingham? That's right: "The residue of thought is memory" (Willingham, 2010). In simplistic terms, this is how students should use Cornell Notes to read critically: First they write notes about facts and details on the right side of the page as they read. The real learning power comes from taking the time after reading to think about what was read and by asking themselves the hard questions like: "What else do I know about this?" "Why?" "Says who?" "Do I believe it?" The left side of the page should contain these questions along with memory cues, sketches, and subject headings. Finally, at the bottom of the page, students summarize what is most important. Using Cornell Notes the right way can help students read critically, which by the way helps them remember what they read.

As we have already seen, the CCSS College and Career Readiness Anchor Standards require a lot of critical thinking, especially in reading. Of the ten anchor standards for reading, half require critical thinking:

1) Read closely to determine what the text says explicitly and to **make logical inferences** from it; cite specific textual evidence when writing or speaking to support conclusions drawn from the text.

4) **Interpret** words and phrases as they are used in a text, including determining technical, connotative, and figurative meanings, and analyze how specific words choices shape meaning or tone.

6) **Assess** how point of view or purpose shapes the content and style of a text.

7) Integrate and **evaluate** content presented in diverse formats and media, including visually and quantitatively, as well as in words.

8) Delineate and **evaluate** the argument and specific claims in a text, including the validity of the reasoning as well as the relevance and sufficiency of the evidence." (bold added; CCSSI, 2010a, p. 35)

The words in bold relate to critical thinking (evaluating the relative merits or faults).

TECHNIQUE: New directions in critical reading. The creation of iBooks 2, a book reading app by Apple, will fundamentally change how students read textbooks. iBooks are not just text on a screen. Students have access to interactive maps, graphs, demonstrations, videos, photo galleries, a search tool, and hypertext definitions. Not only is reading an iBook an engaging multimedia interactive experience, but note taking with the iBook is easier than making flash cards. Students will still have to be able to identify what things should get special attention, but instead of writing in the margins, they will swipe a finger to highlight sections, and then by tapping their fingers, they will quickly attach notes. These notes are collected and can be searched, organized, and reviewed in the notes section as if they were 3 × 5 note cards. The vocabulary of each chapter is already included in the set of electronic note cards, so reviewing vocabulary and notes is a snap.

Ultimately, however, reading critically is more of a *habit of mind* than a reading strategy. It should be the default way of reading for every student. The best way for teachers to teach students to read critically is to read critically with them (remember Mem Fox?). You have to model the kind of thinking that needs to happen as you read a story to your students. Share with students how you are thinking and why you are thinking this way in response to a text (this technique is called metacognition). Now ask students to do the same thing with partners.

After you have done this, when you ask students the hard questions (and don't give them the answers), they can answer them. They can tell you if they believe what the text says is true, and they can tell you why they think so. Once you show students how to read critically, it makes your job as a teacher a lot easier. You can expect students to continue to read critically and think critically on every assignment. You should be prepared for them to keep you on your toes; they might start asking why they have to do the assignment in the first place!

TECHNIQUE SUMMARY: Critical reading. Read 1,000 books with students; have students read with pen in hand (to take notes in the margins of the book or on notepaper); have students use Cornell Notes to think about what they have read; use digital reading (reading using the resources: a hyperdictionary, highlighting, virtual note cards); use metacognition modeling (reading selections out loud and reviewing your thinking and how you react to what you have read while students listen); use the metacognition student version (now students do the same thing with partners).

S T R A T E G Y

Using Questions to Help Students Think Critically

Most of what we currently consider to be "teaching" depends on a teacher's ability to ask questions to students. Research shows that at least 80% of what a teacher does is ask questions (Marzano, Pickering & Pollock, 2001, p. 113). During typical lessons, teachers ask from 30 to 120 questions per hour or 300 to 400 questions per day (Tienken, Goldberg, & DiRocco, 2009, p. 40). But even though many questions are asked, the data shows that typical questioning strategies employed in schools today are ineffective at increasing student learning (Zhang, Lundeberg, McConnell, Koehler, & Eberhardt, 2010, p. 58). Researchers have scratched their heads about this for decades.

Some possible reasons for this anomaly are the following: the questions are not at a sufficient level of rigor; the purpose of the questions is off target; the methods of asking the questions are inadequate; and/or the teachers are simply not experienced enough (Rowe, 1974, 1987; Tienken, Goldberg, & DiRocco, 2009; Albergaria, 2010).

As teachers, we need to come to grips with the fact that we really do not know everything. In the same breath, we can safely say that there is no reason to assume that students know nothing. But perhaps the most important question to ask is, "What does a teacher expect the class to learn from the questioning process? Why ask questions?"

We have to get students to think critically about their own thinking, the textbook, their writing, and everything.

If we look at the dynamics of any classroom, it doesn't take more than a week for students to figure out who is smart, who is not, and who doesn't care. What's worse, studies (Dossett & Burns, 2000) show that after fourth grade, students know how they are perceived and play their roles accordingly. Using questions to help student to think critically can make the classroom environment interesting, lively, and engaging if a few simple techniques are used. The key is to engage as many students as possible. So, we use one of those hook-laden questions that is directed at the entire classroom: "Class, if you could stretch string from here to the moon, how many balls of string would it take?"

The students who know they are not smart are not going to take the bait, and neither will the students who do not care. This leaves the smart kids as the only ones interested in answering, and almost before the question is finished, they have their hands up with an answer, right or wrong. The other two groups of kids are perfectly fine with this routine. Most likely, they are saying to themselves, "Let them answer the questions so I don't have to."

Typically, these are the types of questions that are thrown out to the class as if they were tantalizing treats to be snatched up by all of the eager students. The reality is far different. A teacher may defend this practice because the motivated student who answers will help the whole class learn the answer. That might be true if the whole class were listening, but when the teacher starts pacing the room and stops to ask a question, if students know that the question will be open to the entire class, then most likely two-thirds of the class will not even pay it any attention and will continue doodling or daydreaming.

I spent the day as a first grader, a third grader, a fifth grader, a sixth grader, and a ninth grader. I followed these students to all of their classes. I saw this same sad scenario repeated over and over: the same students answered the questions in every class. From this experience, I discovered something so shocking it was hard to believe. Some students actually went through a whole day—maybe even weeks and months for all I know—and never answered a single verbal question!

Once again, I ask, do we realize how many general questions we throw to the air in the course of a class period? We would be astounded at the results if we simply assigned a student to tally how many of these questions we actually ask each class period. Old habits are hard to break, but students would love to help you break this one.

Let's say we notice this problem and decide something has to change. "Jeffrey," let's name a particular student, "What do John the Baptist and Kermit the Frog have in common?" Several hands slowly recede and all eyes are on Jeffrey. Well, some eyes are on Jeffrey. The rest of the students just breathed sighs of relief that their names were not called. The question asked is not their problem and neither is the answer; both belonged to Jeffrey.

Some teachers may say that while Jeffrey is thinking of the answer, the rest of the students are, too. Wouldn't that be nice? Once again, maybe one-third of the students are thinking about an answer, but the rest are just glad it wasn't them. An easy way to fix this is to appropriately check for understanding.

We ask specific questions to specific students! Most of us have been exposed to the questioning strategies researched by Mary Budd Rowe. She proposed that teachers simply ask a question, such as "What do you call it when an insect kills itself?" pause for at least three seconds, and then say a student's name: "Sally." While the teacher waits, all the students should be automatically thinking about an answer because for all they know, they might be chosen next. Only after another child's name is said will they sigh in frustration because they wanted to answer the question, or sigh with relief because they did not know the answer.

Creative teachers accompany this technique with a system to make sure that every child gets to answer questions in a random fashion. If it is not random, then once they answer a question, they think they have answered their one question and are done for the day. Students figure out pretty quickly that if their name is called, they are off the hook for the rest of class. One way to get around that is to make a show of putting the popsicle stick or tongue depressor back in the same cup with all the other students'. Students will see that they are not off the hook and may still get called on. What they don't know is that you put the popsicle stick with their name on it in the cup upside down so you know that you have already called on them once.

Even with wait-time, only one student is answering questions at one time. The only time it is okay to ask a question to the whole class is when you expect the whole class to answer. Choral answering engages all students, and believe it or not, if you walk around the classroom while students are answering the question all at the same time, you can hear individual answers, and you can tell if they are correct. Interestingly enough, students can tell too, and they self-correct when they realize they are not saying the right answer. The purpose of choral answering is to get all the students to respond—even those reluctant boys. This lowers the affective filter and students feel more comfortable answering the question, whereas if they were the only ones answering the question, they would feel embarrassed. In this way, choral answering builds confidence. A form of choral answering is simply asking students to do something physical, such as touch the right answer, point to the paragraph in their books, stand beneath the poster showing the endoplasmic reticulum, etc. This is called Total Physical Response (TPR) and is an educational version of Simon says. It is a lot of fun for students, as well as for the teacher who thinks of creative ways for students to show that they know the answers—sit on the floor, do the funky chicken, touch the right page with your left elbow, use your chin to point to the word on the wall, etc.

The point of this little side-track into effective questioning is to highlight the importance of engaging all students rather than just a few smart ones. Student engagement is so important because it is impossible to get students to think critically in productive ways if they are thinking critically in unproductive ways. Any questions?

TECHNIQUE SUMMARY: Asking critical thinking questions. Ask questions to specific students and keep track of whom you asked; use wait-time before naming a student; use choral answering to engage all students with whole-class questions; and use Total Physical Response to ask students to do something to show they understand.

TECHNIQUE: Socratic questioning. Socrates had the annoying habit of answering his students' questions with more questions. Part of the College Board's Advanced Placement program teacher training includes the strategy of Socratic Circles. The concept is that you have an inner circle of student experts who have read and studied a text. In an outer circle, student observers watch as the teacher asks the inner circle questions about the text. The teacher must have prepared a list of critical thinking questions rather than fact-based questions because it is nearly impossible to come up with Higher-Order Thinking Skills (HOTS) questions on the fly. This process is great for students who are beginners at critical questioning and who need to spend time observing both the teacher asking questions and the students in the middle answering them. A variation of this is that you eliminate the teacher involvement and assign the students observing to be the ones asking the HOTS questions either in turn or in a creative, random way.

TECHNIQUE: Costa's questions. Students understand more than we give them credit for. (This is a can of worms that some teachers may not want to open, but I think it is for the best.) As teachers, we should be using pre-prepared questions that cause students to think more, and think more critically. Arthur Costa has simplified the six or seven levels of cognitive difficulty defined by Benjamin Bloom. Costa has three levels of questioning: 1. Easy: knowledge-level comprehension questions. 2. Medium: analysis-level questions. 3. Challenging: questions that involve application, synthesis, and evaluation. Teach students the three levels and expect them to identify which level of question is being used. Prepare students to scaffold questions for each other by starting with level-one questions, then going to level-two questions, and finally going to level-three questions. Much like figure skating judges, students can judge the level of the questions by holding up one finger, two fingers, or three fingers as questions are asked in the classroom. This can be a great benefit to the teacher too, because as discussed earlier, far too often teacher questions do not rise above level one. For starters, you might invite students to judge your questions.

S T R A T E G Y

Using Cognitive Dissonance to Help Students Think Critically

You lower yourself down into the cage, and you tie your hand onto the back of the big brown bull, who snorts with anger and irritation as they cinch the rope tight. You are careful to keep your legs from being smashed between the pen wall and the 1,300 pound jittery bull. You are thankful for the cowboy in the front of the bull who is doing his best to distract it from what you are doing. The three other men who are helping you with the ropes and with getting settled on the bull's back encourage you with the words, "Go get 'em, cowboy!" and with pats on the back. Then the gate opens and you hang on for dear life. You know that you must do two things to make the ride worth it: stay on for eight seconds by responding to and anticipating the rhythms of the bull's movements, and show some style in doing it. The world is in slow motion as you experience the longest eight seconds of your life. The bull heaves its bulk into the air, jumps, twists, and cavorts in every imaginable way to get you and that uncomfortable rope off. You realize that your strength is insignificant compared to the near ton of muscle that is throwing you around like a rag doll. You feel like your arm is going to fall off, but you hang on. Seven, eight, the buzzer sounds and you let go of the rope and try to jump free of the angry bull's flailing legs, hooves, and vicious horns. The rodeo clowns get the bull's attention as you dash to safety. After the bull is taken into the pen, you retrieve your hat and your favorite cinching rope from the arena's sandy floor. Only then do you hear the crowd's roar of approval. The thunderous applause with whoops and hollers of appreciation make you stand a little straighter and walk taller. You are just glad to be alive. This time the bull lost.

I took my daughter, Sadie-Belle, to the professional bull riding competition in San Antonio the other day. It was great! This was at the AT&T Center in San Antonio where they normally play basketball, and it was quite a show.

It had been a while since I had watched such an event, and although I have never ridden a bull, I imagine it would be something like I just described.

I noticed that some bull-riders wear helmets instead of hats. Most wear padded, protective vests. They all wear gloves and spurs. But it took me a few moments to figure out what the bull-rider's most valuable piece of equipment really is. It is the cinch rope that each rider carefully went back and retrieved from the stadium floor after each ride. As educators, we have a kind of cinch rope, too.

An Educator's Cinch Rope

What is the purpose of the cinch rope? To the uninitiated, the bulls seem like ferocious animals. The opposite is actually normally the case. For the most part, these bulls are docile, calm creatures. I actually saw one of the bulls lie down in the stocks—refusing to get up for the cowboy to ride him. So how do cowboys get a normally sedentary bull to leap in the air? They tie a cinch rope around the bull's chest, and the bull is so uncomfortable that he is anxious to do anything he can to buck the cowboy off for relief. Keep in mind that bulls are trained to do this and are very successful at it. Out of 40 cowboys who rode, only seven were able to stay on their bulls for the full eight seconds.

A teacher's cinch rope is called cognitive dissonance. The term comes from the concept of different sound waves as they collide, creating disharmonic vibrations. It is uncomfortable to listen to such sour notes. Cognitive dissonance is produced when two ideas seem to collide and only one can be right. The educational cinch rope has to be uncomfortable enough for students to do something about it, and just like the bulls, students need to be trained on how to buck you for causing the dissonance.

In some cases, the information that students have in their brains is incorrect. For example, if you ask a student what causes the seasons of the year, they will likely tell you that it is because the distance from Earth to the sun changes according to Earth's orbital path, when in fact the real reason is that the sun is 20 degrees colder in winter than in summer.

Did I create some dissonance? If I told you that neither of those reasons is true, would you be motivated enough to find out the real answer?[7]

Cognitive dissonance can also be created through the careful gathering and analysis of data to dispel myths, assumptions, and general erroneous beliefs. We have already discussed analytical thinking strategies and tools that help in this regard. Student-led investigations can find answers to questions all students want to know: Does the butter side of the bread always land down? Do blondes have more fun? Does it take only three licks to get to the center of a Tootsie Roll Pop? How many Skittles can fit in my mouth? Seriously, when students ask the critical thinking questions, like how things work and why things work, then they are ready to learn.

TECHNIQUE: Cinch rope. Shel Silverstein was a master at cognitive dissonance. He was able to take normal things we see every day and make us think in different ways about them. That is why we love his poetry and his stories. Data has the capacity to engender cognitive dissonance when critical thinking is applied. Before performing the experiment or data search, students should be required to write what they expect to find. If the data is different, cognitive dissonance ensues. For example, if students in a math class are gathering data about student attitudes and correlating them with right-handedness or left-handedness, this is an opportunity for students to not only graph the data, but also find out what the data is saying and what the implications are, and then ask why the data is the way it is. If students

---

[7]An interesting discussion of the true cause of the seasons can be found at the Annenberg Foundation media website: *www.learner.org/resources/series28.html* (click on the VoD symbol to watch the movie). This is a video produced by the Harvard-Smithsonian Center for Astrophysics in 1987. There are also math and science activities and lessons that go along with this program, called Minds of Our Own and Private Universe.

find out that left-handed people all think the same way, the obvious question is, "Why is that so?"

TECHNIQUE: Says who? Every class has a textbook or a text that is designed to make it easy for students to learn the content of the class. In an effort to do this, textbook authors do a lot of summarizing, and they write as if they themselves are the source of information. To introduce students to the idea of supporting arguments with evidence, have them pick apart one of the chapters in their textbook and identify writing that represents opinion versus writing that requires substantiation.

TECHNIQUE: Critical discussion. Place students in groups of four or five. Give students a topic of discussion that includes a problem to solve or a conclusion to be reached by consensus. Each student has a name tag or a tent card in front of him/her with a statement written on it like the ones in Figure 2.3 (or something similar). Each statement should be displayed clearly so that other students can easily read what it says.

Figure 2.3 Critical Discussion Cue Cards

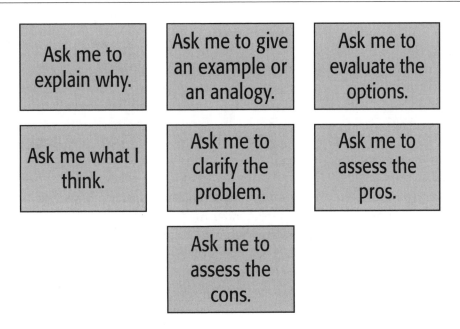

TECHNIQUE: Critical brainstorm. When an author writes a paragraph, several ideas are generated, but only the best ones get down on paper. Critical brainstorms are when you identify the main ideas of a text and then brainstorm on all of the related ideas. In a critical brainstorm, you don't analyze the ideas after all of them are collected, as you would do in regular brainstorms. Instead, you criticize the ideas as soon as they are suggested so that only ideas that withstand scrutiny get written down as options.

TECHNIQUE: HOTS debate. The typical debate format will be used: opposing sides of the same topic, limited time to present an argument and to cross-examine, opening and closing statements, etc. The additional requirement is that only higher-order thinking concepts can be discussed— all evidence must be provided in terms of application, analysis, synthesis, or evaluation. To help train students to do this, you may want to choose just one higher-order thinking task such as evaluation (which is critical thinking). Using the "evaluation" or "critical thinking" as an example, students might prepare an argument on the value, the merits, and the faults of our judicial system. One side would argue the merits and the other would present the faults. This requires students to know something about our legal system and how it works or doesn't work. It also requires students to use all the other higher-order thinking skills to prepare their defense. The arguments themselves should not be just a simple listing of facts, but should identify relative value, merits, and faults. For more advanced groups, the arguments do not have to be polar opposites. You can use the four corners of the room, for example, to identify debate teams. Pick a curriculum-based topic that you know has multiple positions. If you are brave enough, you can allow your students to self-select according to their own beliefs on the topic. In this scenario, two teams debate at the same time, and each team debates three times. So while team A is debating team B, team C is debating team D. Then they switch so team A debates team D and team B debates team C. In the last round, team A debates team C and team B debates team D.

TECHNIQUE: Guess my stance. In this learning activity, the teacher will have prepared position statements on various topics and have written them on stickers. The stickers are then applied to the back of each student. Each student has no idea what is written on the sticker on his or her own back but can read the stickers on the other students. Students are not allowed to tell other students what their stickers say. Care must be taken to warn students not to subvocalize (mouth the words as they read them) as they read any other sticker. Then students must question their classmates regarding what they believe. To begin, restrict students to asking only "yes" or "no" questions. (To get things rolling faster, you can lift this restriction slightly and allow students to answer in sentences as long as none of the words on another student's sticker are used. Students may share examples of what other students believe.) Students will soon learn that trial and error (simply saying, "Do I believe . . . ?") is not the fastest way to identify their position. Students first must identify the topic, and then they must ask questions to identify their stance. If a student had a sticker on his/her back that stated, "I believe that the tenth amendment restricts the federal government's involvement in education," he might approach a fellow student and query, "Does my topic have something to do with the Constitution?" [yes] "Does my topic have something to do with the Bill of Rights?" [no] "Does my topic have something to do with the amendments to the Constitution?" [yes] "Does my topic have something to do with what we discussed in class yesterday?" [yes] "Is my topic about state rights?" [yes] "Do I believe that states should control their own commerce?" [no] "Does my belief have something to do with commerce? [no] "Sovereignty?" [yes] "Education?" [yes] "Can you give me an example of what I believe about education and the tenth amendment?" [You believe that the National Assessment of Educational Progress infringes on state authority.] "Do I believe that states are in charge of their own education services?" [Yes and . . .] "The federal government should stay out of state education!" [Yes—you got it.]

Necessary Teacher Preparations for Critical Thinking

When you read the fine print on a medicine bottle, it can be kind of scary. "If swelling, itching, or loss of eyesight should occur, stop taking this medication immediately and consult your physician." In the fine print, they mention the side effects that may occur from taking the medication. In most cases, the benefits of taking the drug far outweigh the risk of incurring negative or, heaven forbid, harmful side effects. Implementing critical thinking in the classroom is much like taking a medication. Critical thinking can have side effects, and as much as we would like to believe otherwise, these side effects are not all experienced by the students. Teachers also have to deal with those pesky side effects of getting students to think (see Figure 2.4). Teachers have to be prepared to make the necessary adjustments to enable critical thinking as a habit of mind in their students. In order to do so, teachers must accept the fundamental concept that students learn and retain more when they are engaged in critical thinking as expressed in the first part of this critical thinking chapter. In order for students to think critically, teachers have to prepare students with foundational knowledge in the subject area, and then train students to be able to ask and answer critical thinking questions.

Figure 2.4   What Critical Thinking Requires of Teachers

What Critical Thinking Requires of Teachers
It requires teachers to ensure that students have foundational knowledge.
It requires teachers to allocate more time up front for learning and discovering.
It requires more time to prepare effective learning experiences.
It requires facilitator discipline to not give the answer.
It requires teacher patience.
It requires teacher self-confidence.
It requires teachers to be comfortable not knowing the precise outcome of a learning activity.
It requires teachers to redirect challenges.
It requires teachers to admit they do not know.
It requires teachers to be examples of critical thinkers.
It requires teachers to feel comfortable being challenged.
It requires teachers to be resourceful in leaving breadcrumbs for students to find.
It requires a learning-rich environment.

After teaching students to think for themselves, some teachers may believe that they have created a monster. Students are now challenging what the textbook and teacher have to say, questioning the rules and regulations, making suggestions on how to teach and learn, and constantly asking why, why, why. The first step in preparing for this barrage of questions is to remember that the teacher does not have to have all the answers; in fact, it is better to play dumb, even if you do have the answer. Make students find it. The trick for minimizing this uncomfortable feeling is to anticipate it and prepare for it. Another thing that will help is to make sure students understand that it is okay to disagree with someone, but it is not okay to be disagreeable about it.

In the process of planning for lessons either individually or in professional learning community meetings, think of the critical thinking skills that will be necessary to permanently learn the content of the lesson. The Common Core State Standards are a tremendous help in this regard. All of the standards that have to do with assessing, evaluating, choosing, interpreting, distinguishing, etc. have elements of critical thinking. For example, the Mathematical Practices use "reason," "make sense," "construct viable arguments," and "critique," all of which require critical thinking (see Figure 2.5).

Figure 2.5 Mathematical Practices (CCSS, p. 34)

Mathematical Practices
1. Make sense of problems and persevere in solving them.
2. Reason abstractly and quantitatively.
3. Construct viable arguments and critique the reasoning of others.
4. Model with mathematics.
5. Use appropriate tools strategically.
6. Attend to precision.
7. Look for and make use of structure.
8. Look for and express regularity in repeated reasoning.

Once you have determined what you are going to teach, it is time to determine how you will teach it. This is where the CCSS cannot help you. The very first thing you need to do is rough out the lesson and then put yourself in the place of the students. Imagine how students will respond to the learning environment, the learning prompts, and the learning activities. Anticipate student responses to critical thinking and make the necessary adjustments to your lesson. You should know which students to keep away from each other, but more importantly, you should also know which students could inspire in each other new critical thinking skills if they were placed in partnerships or grouped together. As you think "as your students would think," imagine what questions they will have, and steer yourself to not directly answer their questions, but to find ways to reflect the questions back on the students, encouraging them to look in the right locations and seek deeper understanding. Keep the learning responsibility on the shoulders of the students where it belongs. However, you need to be comfortable with not knowing some things, or pretending to not know things. When students are asked to think critically, we may discover that students can come up with the most interesting things, things that we as teachers might not have ever imagined.

Critical thinking is one of the most difficult cognitive activities because it requires the use of evaluation, as well as content knowledge gained from analytical thinking. To be effective learners, students must think critically as they read and as they write. Teachers should make sure that students have enough knowledge and understanding to be able to discuss the content of the lesson, and the critical thinking skills to determine the relative merits and faults of the lesson. Students sometimes need to be elevated to a higher level of interest and urgency. This is more than simply telling students they will be tested on the information. The best way to create interest and urgency is to create a learning environment that requires students to acquire and use their knowledge and skills in order to participate in it. For example, the teacher could prepare a lesson about fractions, but instead of simply drilling students with fraction worksheets, the teacher informs the class that they are going to operate a pizza parlor and sell pizza by the slice for lunch. They have to know how many slices per pizza, and how many total pizzas they will need. In this way, the teacher challenges students' thinking and creates what is known as "cognitive dissonance," or enough of an uncomfortable feeling that will motivate students to do something about it. They will figure it out and in the process learn what fractions are all about.

As a final comment on critical thinking, since teachers spend most of their time asking questions, care must be taken to devise questions that scaffold Costa's Levels of Inquiry (1 easy, 2 medium, and 3 hard) and then utilize these questions in such a way as to help all students, not just the ones listening. These types of questions should be prepared in advance. The easiest way to do this is to prepare a question card to carry with you as you do your direct instruction. Use the question card to prompt you to create questions that not only check for understanding (which is the first level of the scaffold), but also promote higher-order thinking (remember that thinking promotes memory).

Chapter 3

Problem Solvers

Utilizing analytical and critical tools to arrive at solutions

Why Do Students Need to Be Problem Solvers?

I learned something about myself and about students when I was at a "Father and Sons" campout with my son and his friend. One of the fireside activities included a puzzle about which my son and his friend became very curious. The puzzle was the one where a rope is tied around each of your wrists and your partner has a different rope tied around his wrists, but the puzzle is that your ropes are interconnected in the middle. The task is to get separated without untying the ropes from your wrists. The boys witnessed that it could be done, but they did not see how it was done. This piqued their curiosity as a video game could never have done, and they both became determined to figure it out, no matter how long it took.

So Gideon and his friend TJ, who were 15 years old at the time, worked at this puzzle for a good half hour. It was interesting to watch them contort and twist, trying to get the ropes disconnected. Perhaps even more interesting was my reaction to this situation. I knew the answer to the puzzle and part of me desired, more than anything, to share this knowledge. But each time I anxiously asked them if they wanted help, Gideon and TJ were emphatic: "No help!" So I tried unsuccessfully to content myself with holding the flashlight as they tried one idea after another.

While I watched them, I learned a marvelous truth: The motivation to arrive at the solution to the puzzle was far greater than the motivation to receive a candy bar, the prize for solving the puzzle. Considering we are talking about ravenous teenage boys, that discovery is amazing.

As Gideon and TJ continued to work on the puzzle, they noticed that some other boys were doing the same puzzle but were much younger, and their motivation, I believe, was less pure. They wanted the candy bars, unlike Gideon and TJ, to whom the treats were secondary. Worst of all, these younger boys were solving the puzzle (I believe they got help). This only spurred my son and his friend on to more fevered twisting and tangling of ropes while it cankered me that I was not allowed to help. I was anxious to help because I knew the answer. With a few simple words, I could help them be successful.

Then I thought, "Why do I want so badly to share this knowledge? Is it to help them, or is it for me?" I was shocked at the realization that in truth, my motivation was all about me. I wanted to show them how much I knew and how smart I was, more than I wanted them to succeed on their own.

With this realization, I had no trouble keeping my mouth shut, and I let the boys enjoy their learning adventure. A thought did occur to me, though. If I could not help them, perhaps I could get them thinking in the right direction. After all, it was getting late and who knew how much longer it would take them.

I simply asked a question. "How many circles of rope did you say there were?"

"Two!"

"Are you sure?"

"Yes! See! One, t . . . wait a minute. There are . . . four . . . no . . . there are six! Oh, I get it!"

Their progress became much faster and they eventually figured it out. Most importantly, they did it without my help. For these young men, that made all the difference, and it made the victory chocolate that much sweeter.

This experience got me thinking about my teaching. When I slave over a lesson plan and create great questions and conversation points, I sometimes put more value on my knowledge and experience that I want to impart, rather than on the significantly greater knowledge and experience that the students will gain if I let them make discoveries on their own. Then the little devil gets on my shoulder and says, "But that takes more planning and more preparation. It is so much easier just to tell them what they need to learn. After all, why reinvent the wheel?"

Pure discovery is the true "student-centered" strategy. Few teachers have the luxury of allotting all of their time to it. But few will argue that students learn best when they are allowed to discover rather than simply being told. Most often, because of time constraints, teachers only create discovery-learning situations as if they were bubbles in a sea of teacher-centered curriculum. But even then, many teachers feel the need to just give the students the answers—either when students reflexively ask for them, or when the teacher, in frustration, just proffers them when not asked. We forget that reinventing the wheel creates better wheels and smarter students.

I am reminded of the seagulls that forgot how to fish because of hanging around the fishermen. As much as we feel we are being philanthropic with our fish, we are, in fact, feeding our own egos and in essence creating a dependence that will ultimately lead towards intellectual starvation! When teachers constantly answer student questions, we are actually harming the students more than helping them.

The solution is straightforward and at the same time extremely difficult: When we are faced with the temptation to "help" students, we have to be strong enough to CLOSE OUR MOUTHS at the right times! We have to quit saying, "Let me show you." We have to learn to say, "That is interesting. What do you think? Have you thought about this?" And we have to swallow our pride to lie and say, "I don't know. Find out for yourself. You might try looking here." In reality, sometimes we do not know the solution, but that is a dangerous place to remain as an educator.

Not directing and controlling students will be made harder because some students, especially the older ones, will say, "Just tell me what I need to know to pass the test!" You see, our system has trained them to sit quietly and wait for the teacher to give the answers to the predetermined questions. Savvy teachers will have to do some "de-culturalization" and help these students learn how to "discover" on their own before these students will be able to benefit from this method.

Establishing the habit of getting students to ask questions and search for answers takes 21 days, just as it does for any habit. The rewards of this simple change of thinking will endure much longer in the habits of mind we create in our students.

Gideon and TJ had a blast at the Father and Sons outing. They experienced success in learning as they solved the rope puzzle, and because of that, they will be emboldened to tackle even harder challenges. I am glad that I kept my ego in check and did not rob them of that success by selfishly revealing the solution.

Often, mathematics is the main focus of problem solving. The CCSS for mathematics rely heavily on problem solving. Following is just one example of how interwoven problem solving is in each of the Standards for Mathematical Practice:

1. Make sense of problems and persevere in solving them.

Mathematically proficient students **start by explaining** to themselves the meaning of a problem and **looking for entry points to its solution. They analyze** givens, constraints, relationships, and goals. **They make conjectures** about the form and meaning of the solution and plan a solution pathway rather than simply jumping into a solution attempt. **They consider** analogous problems, and try special cases and simpler forms of the original problem in order to gain insight into its solution. **They monitor and evaluate** their progress and change course if necessary. Older students might, depending on the context of the problem, transform algebraic expressions or change the viewing window on their graphing calculator to get the information they need. Mathematically proficient students can explain correspondences between equations, verbal descriptions, tables, and graphs or draw diagrams of important features and relationships, graph data, and search for regularity or trends. Younger students might rely on using concrete objects or pictures to help conceptualize and solve a problem. Mathematically proficient students **check their answers** to problems using a different method, and they continually **ask themselves, "Does this make sense?"** They can understand the approaches of others to solving complex problems and identify correspondences between different approaches. (Emphasis added; CCSSI, 2010b, p. 6)

All of the boldface behaviors in the excerpt relate to problem-solving skills. Note that analytical thinking for arriving at "sense" and critical thinking to "monitor and evaluate" are both required to effectively problem solve. The other seven Standards for Mathematical Practice are designed to support and coincide with the Mathematical Standards for content. As per the introduction, any time a content standard begins with "understand," it is a perfect opportunity to insert the use of Standards for Mathematical Practice. The writers of the CCSS kept the mathematical "content" and the mathematical "practice" separate for two reasons: 1) students (and teachers) who might be a bit weak on a topic may rely too much on the one practice they learn and ignore other ways to solve the problem, and 2) keeping content separate from practice gives teachers flexibility to give students options rather than recipes for solving problems. Once again, the CCSS are not restricting teachers but empowering them to open the floodgates of learning and help students deal with it. This ultimately improves the quality and permanence of learning and, though it might take more effort initially, makes teaching easier in the long run.

Thinking Tools

As you recall, the cognitive scientist Daniel Willingham points out that although human beings are not very good at "thinking" because we depend so much on memory, we love to do it. What we are really good at, however, is making sense of things, even if what we figure out is incorrect (remember Aristotle?). We have a deep need to have explanations for things, even if they are way off base. Remember the movie *Private Universe* from the Annenburg Foundation? The girl in the video had some crazy explanation on how the seasons came about, and it made sense to her. It was wrong, but it explained things in her way of thinking so she felt satisfied. We learned that cognitive dissonance has to occur in order for this wrong thinking to change; otherwise we stick with our first theory.

The first half of effective problem solving is making correct sense of what is going on that is causing the problem. Gaining that understanding requires analytical thinking. The second half of problem solving is determining the causes of the problem and finding solutions. This requires critical thinking (evaluative) and creative (synthesizing) thinking skills. Effective problem solvers use the three thinking tools as a master mechanic uses socket wrenches, screw drivers, and alignment tools. As my father would always tell me, "Use the right tool for the job and the job is easier." Because analytical thinking, critical thinking, and problem solving are not interchangeable tools, knowing their functions will help students match the right thinking tool to the task at hand.

How to Help Students to Become Successful Problem Solvers

Since analytical and critical thinking (essential elements of problem solving) have already been discussed in the how section of this chapter, we will discuss what it takes to arrive at a solution: creativity. Given that we already understand the parts and pieces of a situation and that we have already determined the source of the problem, the only thing left is finding a solution or resolution to the problem. Problem-solving heuristics abound, but all of them have similar formats. In this case, we are focusing on the last few actions of the problem-solving algorithms: identifying options and choosing the best solution. Now that doesn't mean that analysis and criticism are not going to be used anymore; it just means that they are in the background. What brain power is necessary to identify options and possible solutions? Creativity.

Yikes! When the word "creativity" is used, the left side of my head begins to hurt. Why would that happen? Hmm . . . let me see, could it be the years of exposure to right- and left-brain mumbo jumbo? In this book, we are not interested in developing one side or the other of your brain; we want to develop *all* of the brain. This is possible because the brain is a seamlessly integrated whole, and as neuroscientists have discovered, no part of the brain works in isolation. If you want to see some interesting things about the brain, there is an iTunes University course on the brain from the University of Arizona, called Visualizing Human Thought, that shows that even though a man had nearly his entire left hemisphere destroyed by a stroke, including the comprehension (Wernike's area) and speech center (Broca's area), he can still communicate. How? According to right-left brain theories, he shouldn't be able to. Well, what happened was that his brain adapted and found a way to use another part of the brain to take over the job (it is an enthralling story). The point is that thinking—in this case problem solving—is a "whole-brain" activity.

The CCSS' pervasive thread of literacy suggests a way to get to the heart of problem solving. When you say that someone is literate, you are not saying they know how to read. You are saying much more. Being literate means being well-read or having read a lot. Not only that, but there is an assumption that literate individuals have acquired knowledge gained from reading. This knowledge has become part of them and is used both to support and to contradict what this literate person believes or doesn't believe. A literate person, therefore, has ready evidence upon which to base beliefs and sufficient ammunition to argue against other beliefs. In similar fashion, a person charged with solving a problem must have investigated the problem from various angles and sources in order to comprehend the problem and along the way have gathered sufficient evidence to bolster conclusions one way or another about the problem. Following this train of thought, we could call this first stage of problem solving "problem literacy." Thus, being literate about the problem, the individual is ready to creatively find solutions. In chapter 10 we will discuss the three College Readiness literary styles utilized in the CCSS, but for now it is important that we understand that in terms of problem solving, a literate person can read a *narrative* and an *explanatory* piece of literature and accept at face value the information obtained because there is only one side, or only one side is presented. But an *argument* requires a totally different reading skill because the literate person will not concede any points without substantial evidence (and as you will see later in this chapter and in chapter 10, the ability to read arguments effectively is a precursor to writing arguments effectively). The Common Core's point of view is that colleges and universities hold argument as foundational to any study, while mere persuasion is used in advertising and the courtroom. To differentiate the two, an effective argument requires logical evidence to convince a reader, but persuasion may utilize more subtle means, such as authority, expert witnesses, emotions, or the sympathies of the reader to be convincing (CCSSI, 2010c, p. 24).

According to the CCSS, an author is capable of persuading others with arguments because of the amassed knowledge and thinking skills acquired as part of becoming literate. The reader must have similar skills to unravel the arguments and the evidence. In the ACT's report *Reading Between the Lines*, only half of students who took the reading test passed at what the ACT would call the acceptable level. A score of 21 or better means that 85% of those students have a good chance of getting a at least a "C" in history or psychology at a university or college (ACT, 2006, p. 11). I am going to say something earthshattering that no one has ever said before: effective reading is critical for our students to be ready for college and the workforce of today and the future (p. 27).

How does reading an argument help students solve problems? A problem solved must be compelling enough to need a solution. The solution to a problem must be believable, plausible, and doable. An effective solution to a problem is irrefutable because it works! Texts worthy of being read show problems that are solved in intriguing and convoluted ways. These types of texts establish a reason to read them and draw the reader into the situation (I use the word "text" loosely to mean literature as well as explanatory or informational text, narratives, and arguments that have a more academic purpose). Students who learn how to read these types of texts learn how to solve problems from multitudes of perspectives.

Another important thing to consider as we prepare students to be successful in college is the complexity of the literature (text) that they read. According to the CCSS ELA Appendix A (CCSSI, 2010c, p. 2), while the complexity of college reading is rising, the complexity of K–12 reading is diminishing. They quote an ACT report done in 2006 that compares the reading comprehension scores of high school students who did not read complex literature. "The most important implication of this study was that a pedagogy focused only on "higher-order" or "critical" thinking was insufficient to ensure that students were ready for college and careers: what students could read, in terms of its complexity, was at least as important as what they could do with what they read." So it makes sense that as we prepare students with a "higher-order thinking" curriculum, we make sure they are given opportunities to read more complex literature. Complex literature, as defined by the RSVP method (ACT, 2006, p. 15), is shown in Figure 3.1.

Figure 3.1   ACT's RSVP Method for Classifying Complex Literature

Relationships	Interactions among ideas or characters
Richness	Amount and sophistication of information conveyed through data or literary devices
Structure	How the text is organized and how it progresses
Style	Author's tone and use of language
Vocabulary	Author's word choice
Purpose	Author's intent in writing the text

The 2006 ACT study found an interesting fact by looking at the relationship between the complexity of the reading and the test scores on the ACT. Researchers discovered that the more questions a student gets right on the ACT Reading test, the higher their ACT Reading score (a scale of 1–36). Duh, right? What was interesting, though, was what they found when they took those same scores and related them to the complexity of the text. As it turns out, all students with an ACT score under 21 were able to answer correctly about 30% of the questions from a complex text, regardless of their ACT Reading scores. What this means is that students will understand complex texts at the same level, regardless of their other reading skills. Above an ACT Reading score of 21, an exponential relationship develops: as the ACT Reading score increases, the percentage of correctly-answered questions concerning complex texts gradually increases. This signifies that there is a threshold that limits student success on reading-skills tests, and that *obtaining skills in reading complex texts* is the deciding factor. To put it more simply, either students can effectively interpret complex texts or they can't. Once they learn how to effectively read complex texts, only intensive practice will make a difference in their ACT Reading scores. As shown in Figure 3.2, it appears that a score of 21 and above on the ACT Reading test is a reliable predictor of college-readiness and that adequately preparing students to read complex texts can dramatically increase their ACT Reading scores (ACT, 2006, p. 15).

In order to prepare students for college, we as classroom teachers need to get students reading arguments rather than simple narrative, opposing sides of history instead of the myopic textbooks, scientific debates that fueled dis-

Figure 3.2 Relation of Exposure to Complex Literature to Performance on ACT Test

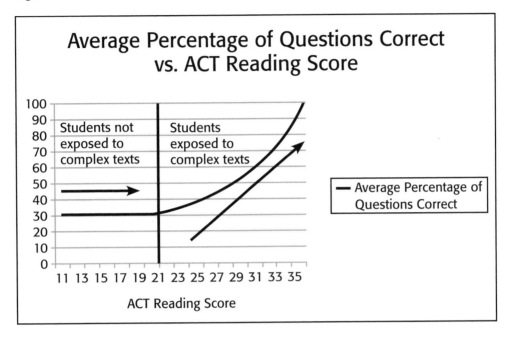

covery, and mathematical disagreements that inspired chaos. The arguments students read must be compelling, believable, and relevant in every subject—and these arguments are out there; we just have to find them.

Now it is time to put all of this all together and relate being literate to being an effective problem solver to being college- and career-ready. In order to solve a problem, students must be literate in the problem—they must have the necessary background information[8] upon which to build an argument of understanding. Then with this knowledge, students can seek solutions. I use the word "solution" deliberately because it relates to effective arguments. My favorite fifth-grade class, at George Gervin Academy in San Antonio, chants and performs hand gestures for a definition to that word that makes sense: A solution is a mixture of two or more compounds that cannot be easily separated. With that definition, the solution to a problem should be so integrated, like the brain (see, I did not forget where this started), that the parts and pieces are not easily separated. The solution is unified or integrated, just like an effective argument.

---

[8]Intriguing information supporting acquiring experience and background knowledge necessary for comprehension through first hand field trips and vicarious field trips, or in other words reading, can be found in Marzano, R. J. (2004). *Building Background Knowledge for Academic Achievement: Research on What Works in Schools*. Alexandria, Virginia: Association for Supervision and Curriculum Development.

Oh, you want an example? Here it goes. One of my favorite books, *The Count of Monte Cristo* by Alexandre Dumas, has all of the RSVP elements of complexity. As far as problem solving, there are several intriguing problems to be solved in the storyline, but Edmond's problem is the biggest. You know the story: just as Edmond was going to have a "happy ever after," everything was stolen from him. The problem: Edmond seeks resolution of his fiendish capture and imprisonment. Then later seeks retribution and revenge? . . . No, it was not retribution; it was just revenge because there was no way to get retribution for the time lost, nor for his happiness, and besides, Edmond is unimaginably rich and has everything he could ever want. Back to the problem—OK, he could have them eliminated (terminated?); that would be the easy solution. Yet, they would not suffer as he had suffered. The real problem with which Edmond wrestled was how to destroy people's lives and make them suffer without killing them. Edmond first had to identify motives for his supposed friends' behavior, and then methods. Why did they move against Edmond in the first place? The answer to that would be fear, envy, greed, and power: fear of being discovered with ties to Bonaparte, envy that Edmond was going to be "captain" and married (in other words—happy), and greed of being able to take Edmond's place and the accompanying monetary possibilities. The final motivation was the mutually beneficial interest in disposing of Edmond to retain power by eliminating loose ends. While Edmond is in prison, he figures this out. In the end, he believes that payback, in all fairness, should be on the same terms. This means that he must take away their happiness, their money, and their power, and in doing all this, make them very afraid. It is easy to look at problem solving in this way, because I know how the story ends.

In the strategies and techniques that follow, I will use literature to help you teach your students effective problem-solving strategies and techniques. (You were probably expecting mathematics or science problems to solve; sorry to disappoint you.) You may agree or disagree, but reading about Edmond's argument is compelling. It is made doable with the incredible fortune he inherited, and as the story unfolds, it is irrefutable—Edmond does what he set out to do. Of course, there are other interesting things to discuss about this story: Is the terrifying transformation of Edmond worth the cost? Does Edmond not become what he is trying to destroy? You get the drift.

S T R A T E G Y

Methods for Inciting Creativity and Identifying Options for Solving Problems

Wouldn't it be nice if we had a creativity pill full of playfulness, irreverence, rule-bending, and flubber[9] every time we needed creativity to solve a problem? The thing about creativity is that it is not like recalling a fact or remembering a situation. Though like memory, it requires intense mental effort that is directed at a problem, unlike memory, there is no guarantee the effort will produce results. With problem solving, sometimes we have creativity forced upon us. Dire circumstances and desperation can make us creative. Other times, responding to less critical motivators such as peer pressure, laziness, ambition, and shame can inspire creativity. But most of all, being creative means coming up with a variety of options from which we can choose to go about solving problems, for whatever reason. But these options are not pulled out of thin air. Our personal experiences, memories, knowledge of the situation, and knowledge of similar situations all affect our ability to engage creativity to devise options for solving a problem. The more options that are created, the more opportunities we will have for successful resolution of the problem. The following techniques are shared to identify problem-solving options but can also be used for other creative learning opportunities with a little adjustment. Most of the techniques for teaching this strategy are take-offs on what we call brainstorming for solutions.

TECHNIQUE: Brainstorming with a twist. Brainstorming is best when it is done in groups of four or five students with the strict rule that no filtering is to occur. Okay, a little bit of filtering should be allowed for inappropriate words and topics, but other than that, everything is written

---

[9] Remember that series of Walt Disney movies about the "Absent-Minded Professor" (1961), played by Fred MacMurray? He accidentally invents "flubber" and finds a lot of interesting things that can be done with it. He puts it on the basketball team shoes, he puts it on the football, and he even puts it in his car to make it fly. Robin Williams starred in a remake of it (1997), but it was not nearly as good as the original.

down and accepted. After having read Roald Dahl's story, *The Witches*, a fourth-grade class might start brainstorming about the topic: "If you are a witch, how could you hide who you really are?" Give students two minutes to write down everything they can think of (this works with individuals, pairs, or groups of four or five). The teacher then puts a twist on the thinking: "Which of your ideas would work when you are on the beach? when you are on a tennis court? when you are at Disneyland? Which ideas would you have to change? Any other ideas come to mind?"

TECHNIQUE: Word association. This is a variation of a couple of popular word games called Boggle and Password. The point of the game is to come up with as many unique words related to the word in question as possible. A sixth-grade teacher would flash a word on the screen from a great book, let's say *Belle Prater's Boy* by Ruth White, that has just been read. The topic is "Why does Woodrow tell stories?" The students in teams of two to four have to come up with as many related words or phrases from the book as possible. Examples: "They're funny," "They're scary," "They're short." After students run out of easy words, they have to think harder: "true," "make-believe," "he likes fairytales," "he's sad," "to make fun of," "he lies," "to make Gypsy happy," "mother's ghost," "he's afraid," "for protection," "he's like his mother." Students have only one minute. After the time is up, the teams one by one share the words they have written down. As a word or phrase is read, if another group has it, then everyone has to scratch it out. If no one has the word or phrase, and the class agrees that it is related to the topic, everyone circles it. After the last team has read their words, then the team with the most unique words wins.

TECHNIQUE: Inkblot (Rorschach) test. This is more of an arts and crafts type of creativity technique. Students make spots of ink (several colors work best) on paper and fold the paper in half, squishing it completely flat. Then they open the paper and write a paragraph or two on what they see from various angles. To make this more interesting, the teacher chooses a book or story, like Edgar Allen Poe's "Cask of Amontillado," and students have to come up with at least four different icons of the story related to their inkblot. For each icon, students should describe how it connects to the story. Examples: "motivation," "humiliation," "enticement of the cask," "fear of the catacombs," "humor the jester," "revenge of Montressor." Another twist would be to take the perspective of one of the characters and try to determine how he or she would interpret the inkblot, or take the perspective of the author and how he or she would interpret the inkblot.

TECHNIQUE: *Astronomer's view.* This technique is taking the birds' eye view to its logical limit The point is to look for patterns (constellations) in the surrounding stars. Many times solutions appear as we step back from the problem (way back) and identify the big picture and what is around it. To do this, we need to ask questions like, "Why was the book written?" "What did the author want from readers?" "Who did the author think would read this book?" "What other books are like this one?" "How did the author's life affect his writing?" In *Journey to the Center of the Earth* by Jules Verne, some of the big pictures are these: "Back in Mr. Verne's time, did they believe that it was possible to have a world at the center of the earth?" "What did they know about dinosaurs back then compared to what we know now?" "What other books did Jules Verne write?" "Why are all of Jules Verne's books adventures?" "Was Jules Verne describing his own time period accurately, or was that the future for him?" "What did Verne think about the future?" "What options did Jules Verne have to solve the problems he presented in his book?" "How have those options changed?" Depending on the age of your students, you could either ask the questions yourself and put them on a webquest page for students to investigate, or teach the technique and have students ask the astronomer questions and then answer their own questions.

TECHNIQUE: *Atomic view.* The atomic view looks at a story through the eyes of an electron microscope into the very structure of the words spinning madly around the ideas. Students look at word choice, style, spelling, rhythms, meter, and fluency in order to elucidate possible meanings and motives of the author. For example, *A Connecticut Yankee in King Arthur's Court* by Mark Twain deals with two colliding time periods. Sophomore English classes could list the words used by the "Boss" and then list the vocabulary of the knights and make some stunning conclusions. By asking, posing, or providing questions like the following, even more discussion about word choice and intended interpretation would ensue: "How did the Boss overcome the difficulty of describing something with which he was very familiar, but the knights knew nothing about because it hadn't been invented yet?" "What part did the culture play in not only the choice of words used but also in how those words were placed in sentences (rhythms, meter, phraseology)?" "Some of the words used by the knights were old English and not used in modern language; how did Twain write so readers would understand them?" "How did Twain illustrate the thinking, ideology, and culture of the people in the time of Camelot?" "What level of language did Twain use to narrate the story?" Students could create a spreadsheet of the different language characteristics of each type of individual in the story in order to compare and categorize the words used. They could demonstrate how Twain effectively or ineffectively represented different castes and education levels among the people of Camelot.

TECHNIQUE: Bubble test. Just as the name suggests, this technique gathers what floats to the top first and then categorizes the ideas as they come along. Through a group histogram (frequency analysis), we can determine which bubbles are larger in terms of priority or popularity than others by how many groups come up with the same idea. This can be done as a group activity or individually, but it is more fun in a group. If the book that is being read in a fifth-grade class is *Baseball in April and Other Stories* by Gary Soto, then each group can take a chapter and identify the problems encountered by Alfonzo, Hector, Michael, and Veronica. Students could then identify the solutions in groups, then add their conclusions to the whiteboard histogram.

TECHNIQUE: Gallery walk. Each group of four or five students creates a poster representing the best symbolism of the literature. For example, eighth graders would be able to identify the problems (plots) and the effectiveness of the solutions in the story *The War of the Worlds* by H. G. Wells. For example: "Confronted with the reality that man is insignificant compared to more advanced beings," "Fear of being caught and the motivation of survival," "Human desire to fight back against impossible odds," "Witness the metamorphosis of humanity when placed in dire circumstances," "Revelation of what is most important in this life," "Struggling with despair." Once the posters are displayed on the walls, each group stands up and travels about the room, critiquing each poster. On sticky notes, each group writes a question or makes a comment. After all the posters have been reviewed, each group looks at the comments and writes a reflection about what they learned by reviewing other posters, and what they learned by reading the comments and questions of the other groups.

TECHNIQUE: Flashlight. Wherever the light shines (use a light that can focus the beam), that is the point of interest. T. H. White's *The Sword in the Stone* in *The Once and Future King* is perfect opportunity to use this technique. Let's shine the light on Merlyn. Merlyn's problem was how to make Wart into the king that Merlyn knew he would be. Similar to the game of Jeopardy, Merlyn had the answers, but he did not have the questions because he hadn't asked them yet. If you recall, Merlyn was the first Benjamin Button[10] and lived his life backwards (actually, T.H. White published his book in 1958, while F. Scott Fitzgerald published his in 1922, so it is the other way around, but you understand what I mean). While the light is shining on Merlyn, students identify the problems he had in training Wart, his difficulties with Sir Ector, etc. Then the teacher (or student) shines the light on Kay. Students now identify what problems Kay had to overcome to become a knight, how he dealt with the strange Wart, and how he overcame his shock when Wart was able to pull the sword out of the stone and he could not. The light could land on King Pellinore, or Archimedes, or the pike.

TECHNIQUE: Solute vs. solution. A solution is like water and sugar. Once they are mixed, they are not easily separated. They become a single unit. The solute is what is being dissolved, the sugar; the solvent is what does the dissolving, the water. Students' task is to identify the elements of the literature that are so intertwined as to be viewed as a single element, when in fact they are multiple elements. Shakespeare was a master at weaving different parts of his plays with different elements that seem to flow together. Perhaps the best example of this is *A Midsummer Night's Dream*, in which reality and surrealism exist seamlessly in the same space.

---

[10] "The Curious Case of Benjamin Button" is an intriguing story in F. Scott Fitzgerald's book *Tales of the Jazz Age.* In 2007, "The Curious Case of Benjamin Button" was made into a movie (www.imdb.com/title/tt0421715/) in which Brad Pitt played the tragic Benjamin Button. You can read the short story at www.readbookonline.net/read/690/10628/

SECTION I
CONCLUSION

Thinking Can Be an Unbelievably Satisfying Learning Experience

I ask my junior-high-aged daughter, Mercedes, "How was school?" I have learned to not ask yes or no questions, but she still gives me a one-word answer: "Good." My typical reply is, "Good for what?" This makes her laugh, but she still doesn't want to provide much detail about the day's learning activities. It might be that she is providing a buffer of protection for her teachers from an overly critical dad, or I suppose it could be a junior-high-aged syndrome—simply not wanting dad to know too much. Whatever it is, "Good" is her typical response, and she only shares more after insistent prodding. It would be nice if I asked, "How was school?" and she responded, "Unbelievably satisfying!"

Those are words that I don't think are regularly used to describe schools. Even more specifically, I am reasonably certain that in the history of the world, no student has ever described her day at school as "unbelievably satisfying." These are the thoughts that pass through my head every day as I drive past a billboard for Dr. Pepper, in which a smiling leprechaun holds up a soda can and in big bold letters states, "Unbelievably Satisfying!" But wouldn't it be awesome if schools were able to inspire this kind of emotion in students?

So how could a regular, everyday school experience be unbelievably satisfying to a student? Dr. Pepper claims it is unbelievably satisfying because it quenches a thirst, it is sweet, it is tasty, and it is fizzy. Let's look at how a teacher can make his or her learning activities unbelievably satisfying for students. Students have a general curiosity, a thirst to find out what's new. When a teacher inspires students to discover something new, you can actually hear the "gulp, gulp, gulp—ahhhhhhh." Students love to feel needed and essential. When teachers share leadership and play to the strengths of the student, there it goes again: "gulp, gulp, gulp—ahhhhhhh." Students crave honest and specific praise, and when they get it from an observant teacher, "gulp, gulp, gulp—ahhhhhhh." The sweetness of victory fills students to the brim when they succeed at difficult problems with which an astute teacher has challenged them: "gulp, gulp, gulp—ahhhhhhh." Canny teachers purposefully engage students in hands-on projects designed to leave students with a taste for more, while energetic and enthusiastic teachers create fun and active learning environments where students' excitement can't help but bubble to the surface, "gulp, gulp, gulp—ahhhhhhh." That is how teachers can create unbelievably satisfying days at school for students.

Students need to feel like they are part of something extraordinary. Certainly, school is hard work, but it doesn't have to be ordinary. We have explored ways in which learning using analytical thinking, critical thinking and problem solving can make the learning experience extraordinary and "unbelievably satisfying." The CCSS help teachers focus on these three important elements of literacy and mathematics that allow teachers to encourage deeper learning rather than wider learning (that's only an inch deep).

Getting away from the idea that education is something you do to kids, and embracing the idea that it is something to be experienced *with* kids, is what will make the difference between a "good" day at school and an "unbelievably satisfying" day at school. Mercedes is my youngest child, but I have hope that soon she will have unbelievably satisfying days at school every day.

Section II

Creating College- and Career-Ready Learners

What Is a Learner?

 In this section, I would like to explore what a college-ready learner looks like. The list of essential questions in Figure II.1 forms the basis of the habits of mind that we seek to develop in college-ready learners. The CCSS define a college- and career-ready learner in seven ways: has independence; has strong content knowledge; has the ability to adapt to audience, task, purpose, and discipline; has the ability to comprehend and critique; values evidence; uses technology and digital media; and has appreciation for perspectives and cultures (see Figure II.2).

Figure II.1 Habits of Mind at Central Park East Secondary School

Central Park East Secondary School's Habits of Mind, as Described by Deborah Meier in *The Power of Their Ideas*

- The question of evidence, or "How do we know what we know?"
- The question of viewpoint in all its multiplicity, or "Who's speaking?"
- The search for connection and patterns, or "What causes what?"
- Supposition, or "How might things have been different?"
- Why any of it matters, or "Who cares?"

Source: http://www.essentialschools.org/resources/521

What is a learner? A learner is a natural observer and mimic. From the time of birth to the age of two, a child is a learning prodigy. Think of what is learned during that time. We learn to manipulate and control our bodies to the extent that we can walk, move about, and run. We learn to recognize and respond to audio, visual, and sensory stimuli. We learn to use our senses

Figure. II.2 College- and Career-Ready Learners (CCSSI, 2010a, p. 7)

Independence	Strong Content Knowledge	Adapt to Audience, Task, Purpose, and Discipline	Comprehend and Critique	Value and Evidence	Technology and Digital Media	Prespectives and Cultures
Comprehend and evaluate complex texts	Base of knowledge across a wide range of subject matter	Adapt their communication	Engaged and open-minded— but discerning— readers and listeners	Cite specific evidence when offering an oral or written interpretation	Enhance their reading, writing, speaking, listening, and language use	Appreciate widely divergent cultures
Construct effective arguments and convey intricate or multifaceted info	Proficient in new areas through research and study	Adjust purpose for reading, writing, speaking, listening, & language use	Appreciate nuances: audience, tone, & connotations affect meaning	Use relevant evidence when supporting their own points in writing and speaking	Tailor their searches online to acquire useful info	Learn and work together
Discern a speaker's key points, request clarification	Read and listen to gain both general knowledge and discipline-specific expertise		Know that different disciplines call for different types of evidence	Make their reasoning clear to the reader or listener	Integrate what they learn using technology with what they learn offline	Understand other perspectives through reading and listening
Build on others' ideas, communicate their own ideas	Refine and share their knowledge through writing and speaking		Understand precisely what an author or speaker is saying	Constructively evaluate others' use of evidence	Know strengths and limitations of various technological tools and mediums	Communicate effectively
Use a wide-ranging vocabulary			Question an author's or speaker's assumptions and premises		Select and use those best suited to their communiction goals	Evaluate other points of view critically and constructively
Self-directed learners seeking out and using resources			Assess the veracity of claims and the soundness of reasoning			Vicariously have experiences much different than their own

(mainly our mouths) to explore and discover the world we live in. The most amazing thing we learn is how to communicate. Research shows that babies zero to eight months old, though they are not able to communicate effectively, are busy cataloguing language cues. By the time they are 11 months old, they recognize their native language from other languages and are able to differentiate the native sounds and ignore the non-native ones (Conboy, Sommerville, & Kuhl, 2008). For example, in English "ra" and "la" are different sounds because English uses a lot of r's and l's, but in Japanese, these two sounds are identical because the Japanese don't really use either sound.

If you want to see an amazing video, watch Dr. Kuhl, from the University of Washington, describe how children learn languages from six to eight months old.[11] Dr. Kuhl points out that "natural" language learning skills drop off after seven years old. That doesn't mean we cannot learn other languages; it just means that our native language will get more and more in the way as we do. So, from birth, we are learning experts who learn by the observation and mimicry of the people in our lives.

What is a learner? A learner remembers what he or she learns. Could we say a learner is a rememberer? Yes, but that doesn't quite cover it, because I believe the learner wants to learn and not just remember. The act of learning is part of that desire. As we mature, we learn (and remember what we learn) more and more by exploration and discovery. We learn with hands-on and minds-on. We learn in the situation, in the moment, and in the locale. Unsurprisingly, this type of memory is called locale memory and is instant memory (Caine, & Caine, 1991). For example, we all remember what we were doing on 9/11. So we learn instantly by experiencing events that are important to us.

What is a learner? A lover of stories. We (especially as children) love to listen to and tell stories. Daniel Willingham, a cognitive scientist and, as it turns out, a fellow Star Wars enthusiast, explains that we can easily remember complex storylines from movies or television shows that we have seen just one time (it really helps if the story is engaging, like Star Wars!) (2010, p. 51). Using Star Wars as a story example, Willingham goes on to describe the four c's that serve as a foundation for any worthy story: causality, conflict, complications, and character (see Figure II.3)— all held together by action (p. 52). So we easily learn content in the action and adventure of the story structure, all the while learning the facts and the complex concepts required for argument.

What is a learner? A learner is a linguist capable of mimicking inflection, tone, and accent. A learner is a student in my class naturally copying the language of the teacher. As the teacher, I can tap into the student's natural ability and affinity to learn language by helping him or her learn the scientific vocabulary, capitalizing on the fact that the mouth is part of his or her natural language learning toolbox, directly connected to the brain. (There is no way students can remember a word if they can't say the word.) Spoken learning is powerful.

---

[11] They have a new machine called a MEG (magnetoencephalography) which is different from CAT scans and MRIs. It is silent and does not require the subject to remain perfectly still, meaning it will not scare babies, and they can be awake while the testing is going on. There are other cool things about this machine, but the MEG opens up totally new horizons in learning how we learn. This is the link to the YouTube video: (www.youtube.com/watch?v=qRRiWg6 wYXw&feature=list_related&playnext=1&list=SPED2FC89AE6EFE8F8)

Figure II.3   Essential Story Elements

What is a learner? A learner is a problem solver, someone who can put all the learning and cognitive skills to use to find a solution. As her teacher, I can augment a student's inclination to learn by creating learning situations that require her to discover the reason pi equals 3.14 all by herself (this is inquiry). As her teacher, I can foment the incredible instant memory of stories by helping her to think about the "meaning" by telling the story of Pearl Harbor using the four c's. As her teacher, I can provide opportunities to train her mouth as well as her brain. I can change the venue of learning, transform my classroom, or change the rules to create new locales for long-term learning. Most of all, I can inspire her to understand that the learner is the protagonist of learning, not merely the product of learning.

Inquisitive Learners

Inquisitiveness: Curiosity about surroundings,
constantly asking questions: Why? How?

Why Should Students Have an Inquisitive Nature?

The other day, I walked into a Walgreens store looking to refill some medicine. Of course, they put the pharmacy way in the back so that unsuspecting customers looking to fill prescriptions or find medicine have to walk by all the other items that are enticingly displayed along the way. I was walking down one of those aisles and caught a glimpse of a mason jar with a butterfly in it. The packaging of the jar pointed to a button that was labeled "Press Here." So I did. The plastic-winged butterfly began to flutter as if it had just been caught, and then settled down, slowly opening and closing its wings—just like a real butterfly would do. Did I just walk away and say, "That's cute"? Nope, I was curious how the butterfly was made to work that way. So I looked more closely to analyze the mechanism as I pushed the "Press Here" button several times. (This, by the way, is why you never want to select the first item in the pile to buy.) I found out that it is quite an ingenious device, based on a simple principle. Are you curious as to how it works?[12]

In the Common Core State Standards, there are really only two strands: English Language Arts and Mathematics. Some might say, "What about

---

[12] To satisfy your curiosity, go to this website: www.mybutterflyinajar.com/retailers-for-butterfly

science and history?" Let's start with history. In order to interact with the content of history, what options do students have? They can talk to someone who has lived history, they can watch a movie about history, they can read about history, they can speak about history, and they can write about history. All of these activities require literacy skills. Without the effective literacy skills that the CCSS propose, students would not be able to interact with history at the college and career level. The same learning characteristics we have already discussed with analytical thinking, critical thinking, and problem solving apply to literacy in any content area, including history. Now let's consider science. The bottom line for a scientist is to be inquisitive about things, to perform experiments, and to discover things. Well, that is the simplified version of science, but just as with history, students must be adept at reading, writing, and conversing about science. Much of scientific research is done beginning in the library, first understanding the achievements and discoveries of others and then finding out what needs more substantiation and what is still unknown. English language arts are therefore the foundation of scientific learning and understanding, hence the literacy foundation in the CCSS.

Isn't science in its own category in terms of learning? Not necessarily. We often hear of math and science sort of lumped together, but this may be because the two are challenging and difficult subjects for many people. Science learning depends on math learning, but not necessarily the other way around. A teacher quality program at Texas State University called Mix It Up[13] is trying to help teachers connect math and science conceptually and pedagogically. The premise is that public school science teachers understand the hands-on methods of laboratory experiments, but may be a little shaky on the math concepts, while math teachers teach mathematical procedures but might need help in making the math relevant. This is where the Mix It Up program sees its opportunity. Dr. Sandra Moody-West and her team bring math and science teachers together and have them learn advanced math and science concepts conceptually. Then the two have to prepare and teach a correlated math and science lesson. Through this practice, Dr. Moody-West has seen math teachers integrate their learning activities with science teachers in the participating schools, and as a result, student understanding of math and science has increased. Dr. Moody-West, who is a biologist, will tell you that teaching science and math requires a lot of English language arts.

The reading standards for science begin in the sixth grade and are composed of the same four categories for all reading subjects (isn't that nice—

---

[13] Take a look at Mix It Up at Texas State University in San Marcos: www.cose.txstate.edu/mathematics

some uniformity that actually makes it easier to remember and apply the standards?): *Key Ideas and Details, Craft and Structure, Integration of Knowledge and Ideas* and *Range of Reading and Level of Text Complexity.* The ten descriptors for Reading Science parallel the Reading Standards for Informational Text with one obvious difference—under *Key Ideas and Details,* students are to be able to read instructions and follow them in increasing levels of precision and complexity. Being able to follow written instructions is a valuable skill for college- and career-readiness.

How to Help Students Develop an Inquisitive Nature

Having an inquisitive nature was one of the characteristics of a college- or career-ready student, according to 400 university professors in Dr. Conley's 2003 landmark study. Higher education encourages curiosity, much more than EC-12 public education, except for perhaps Montessori schools, but public school children need it just as much as college students, if not more because they have more to learn. Luckily, as discussed earlier, children are naturally curious and it follows that students should be also. I have never seen a student who was not curious about something. While I have seen a few students who have suppressed their curiosity when they enter school to such an extent as to be nearly undetectable, their curiosity is still there—which means that given the right circumstances, it can be revived. Human beings are hard-wired to be curious from birth, and being curious is a major activity of childhood and young adulthood (and yet recently, more and more students would rather be curious-looking, as evidenced by popular clothing styles).

So if we notice students are not as curious in our classes as they should be, then we should first look at what we are doing, or not doing, that might cause this to happen. Of course, I have some suggestions of places to inspect first (see Figure 4.1).

If the answer to any of the questions is no, then getting students to be curious again is a relatively easy fix—just change what we are doing or not doing. If all of the answers are yes, then the fix is still possible, but we have to be more patient. One of the foundational instructional methods for inciting curiosity is called inquiry. I need to caution you before we go further into inquiry. The first caution is that inquiry is ideal for situations that can be discovered and explored. A science teacher would never use inquiry as an instructional method to teach students safety. The best method for teaching lab safety is direct instruction (Madeline Hunter's [1994] seven-step lesson plan, for example). The second caution is that in trying to get students to participate fully

Figure 4.1 Condtitions Necessary to Foment Curiousity

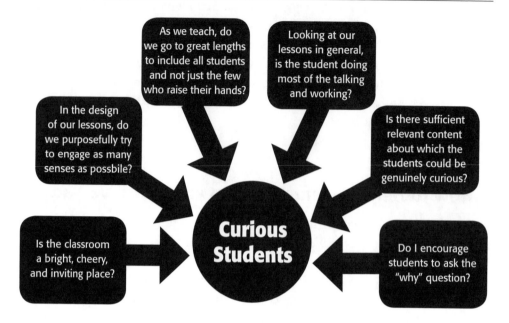

in the inquiry process, we have to remember that most likely, they have been conditioned to do the opposite of inquiry—shut up and listen. Depending on the severity of the case, it may take a while to get them "unconditioned."

As an example of this, several years ago, I was involved with the Ford PAS[14] program, which has an awesome business/STEM inquiry-based curriculum. We brought in thirty ninth graders, from three different schools, for a nine-week summer course. The first week that students were presented with the inquiry lessons, they did not know what to do. They just sat there silently. The Ford PAS folks had anticipated this and created a course to help student learn how to do inquiry. Since the summer program instructors had the students all day long, for the first week they used this introductory lesson and basically trained students how to ask questions, brainstorm solutions, collaborate with their groups, and investigate possibilities. You would not have recognized the groups after nine weeks. No one had to tell them to ask clarifying questions, critically analyze, or research; it was automatic. And instead of silence, an energetic buzz of conversation abounded when they were given their final assignment.

---

[14] This is an interesting STEM/business leadership oriented program funded by the Ford Motor Company Fund (not the Ford Foundation). www.fordpas.org

My point in sharing this is that if you are just starting inquiry, and have all of your other teaching ducks in order, then just be patient and for heaven's sake, don't freak out because of "silence" in the first inquiry lesson. You have to be willing to let students fail a few times before they get it. Students are smart, and they will remember what it is like to be intellectually curious, and they will appreciate the liberty that you are giving them. The most important thing about inquiry is that the learning scenario you set up must be compelling enough for students to become engaged.

You may object by saying, "But I don't have time to play games or do projects (or allow students to be curious). I have to teach them (drill them) on the content of the state standardized tests!"

I may quip, "So . . . ? Why is that your problem? The students are the ones who have to take the test; let them worry about it."

You may counter, "You don't get it. I am judged by how well my students perform on these state tests.[15] I seriously don't have time to do the fun stuff."

I most likely will reply sarcastically, "Oh, so you get graded on how well your students perform, but you do not want your students to learn in the best way possible?"

With all of this pressure on students to perform well on standardized tests, we must understand that it is in our best interest to help students reignite their curiosity and interest in learning. We have to agree that the so-called higher order "fun stuff" is not just fluff that can be discarded for lack of time; it is at the very core of how and why we learn at all. In the final analysis, the "fun stuff" will make teaching and learning easier and more enjoyable for everybody, and as a direct result of this, your students will remember more!

As mentioned earlier, Mr. Willingham (2010) gets to the crux of the matter right away: It is not the state testing that is doing the damage to "education." It is the teacher's reflexive response to state testing that is causing the problem. Too many teachers assume that the best and quickest way to get information into students' brains is to tell them what they should know and then expect them to know it. Mr. Willingham introduces the concept that "Memory is the

---

[15] Just so you understand where I come from, I believe that there are many things in the current educational system that need to be changed; however, state standardized testing is not one of them. I firmly believe that NCLB, although not perfect, is a great step in the right direction. I believe this because I have seen administrators and teachers who previously were only concerned about local grades and behavior for some students and now are concerned with all students actually learning something. Although we have a long way to go, at least the state standardized testing sets minimum standards for teachers to attain (notice I did not say students—once the students are accountable, then we will see great improvements). The main hurdle now is to get teachers to quit teaching right up to the minimum standards and instead to inspire learning beyond them.

residue of thought" (p. 41). This means that we remember most what we think about most. If the students are interested and inspired to think about things for prolonged periods, then memory is enhanced. This is where inquiry, constructivism, and curiosity come into play, providing opportunities for students to think about what they are learning. In this way, memory is improved, students do better on standardized tests, and . . . guess what? Students enjoy learning! Problem solved.

Memory is the residue of thought.

(WILLINGHAM)

S T R A T E G Y

Anticipatory Set[16]

The success of a lesson has much to do with the way it starts. Madeline Hunter knew this when she created the seven-step direct instruction lesson plan. The very first step is what she termed the Anticipatory Set (see Figure 4.2). Others may call it the "hook" or the introduction to the lesson. With students as sophisticated as they are, the anticipatory set has to be more than simply telling students what lesson is about. At the beginning of a lesson, teachers have a few critical moments when students' natural curiosity overpowers other interests. Lessons should start off with something that grabs student's attention and doesn't let it go for fifty-five minutes. The anticipatory set also has another function. It firmly puts the teacher in the driver's seat (after all, it is a direct teach model) and reinforces the concept that the teacher has something urgent that students want.

---

[16] Dr. Madline Hunter established the direct instruction method in the early 80s, and it is still the foundation of direct instruction today. The seven steps are Anticipatory Set, Input, Modeling, Checking for Understanding, Guided Practice, Independent Practice, and Evaluation (a good template can be found at http://template.aea267.iowapages.org/lessonplan). Make no mistake, direct instruction using the Hunter seven-step lesson plan is effective (Schmoker, 2011; Steward, Martin, Burns, & Bush, 2010). In fact, Dr. Michael Schmoker, in his book *Focus*, establishes that if teachers consistently used this method, tremendous progress would be made toward student achievement (2011).

Figure 4.2 Two Purposes of the Anticipatory Set

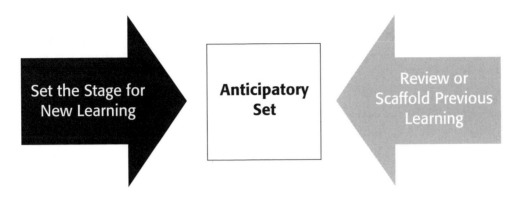

As demonstrated by the CCSS' focus on literacy regardless of content, we can follow suit and approach the anticipatory set from a literature point of view. Much as a good story teller fabricates a new world with words, the teacher must set the learning stage before the main action, climax, and ultimate dénouement (I had to look this word up—it means unraveling of the plot) of the lesson can occur. (You recall that Willingham suggested that every lesson be told as a story in order for the students to have instant recall.) As teachers, you have two possible objectives of anticipatory sets: An introduction setting the stage for a lesson and building a conceptual framework into which the new learning of the lesson can be placed, or the expansion, review, or scaffolding of previously-learned content. One of the exciting things about teaching and learning is that every day there are brand new opportunities to teach and learn that no amount of planning can anticipate, but having the anticipatory set helps the lesson get off on the right foot. A creative teacher can easily prepare lessons with something stunning and new to surprise or even shock students into alertness in the anticipatory set. The more you do this, the more firmly you establish a routine. Students (as well as teachers) are creatures of habit, and behavioristic conditioning works. If you have something interesting at the beginning of each class period, students will begin to expect it, and they will adjust their behavior to take advantage of it. I hope that the following techniques will give you some ideas for keeping students on their toes.

TECHNIQUE: Sponge. The sponge is a tried and true instructional strategy that serves multiple purposes. It is called a sponge because it soaks up the wasted time at the beginning of a class while the teacher takes roll or passes back papers. Some call it a bell-ringer; others may call it the warm-up, flashback, or lesson opener. The most useful purpose is to get students busy and productive while the teacher takes care of attendance and getting the lesson started. It also sends a message to the students that their time is valuable enough for the teacher to not waste any of it. It establishes a sense of urgency and importance of the learning work done in the classroom, and it diminishes down time that can allow behavior issues to arise. Just like the anticipatory set, it can serve as a review of prior material, or it can set the stage for learning new material. It must be something that students can perform independently, without the aid of the teacher (remember the teacher is busy taking roll, accepting and recording homework, counting school lunches, etc.).

The first five minutes of class is a perfect time to give pretests before a new concept is taught, or a short quiz to reinforce recall of important facts. The sponge activity needs to be something that students do not need the teacher to help them to do, because the teacher will be busy taking attendance, doing a lunch count, etc. Also, the sponge activity needs to be ready to go before students begin arriving in class. As students walk in, their eyes will be drawn to the whiteboard, overhead, chalkboard, or other display where they will have their independent work instructions for the next five minutes. It is important to set a time limit and stick to it (no more than five minutes). Then, to establish that the sponge is valuable learning, connect the sponge to the lesson at hand. For example, in chapter one I shared with you that as a Spanish language teacher, my job was to help students read and write in Spanish. What I didn't share was that I also had the task of teaching reading and writing in the language in which other students already had native fluency. To help these students, I used Spanish sayings called *dichos* to help my students think abstractly, to learn about their culture, and to interact with the words in Spanish. As they came into class, they wrote down the *dicho* in their journals, and in Spanish gave an application of the *dicho*, while I took roll and checked homework. Other examples of effective sponge activities follow.

- ◆ **Science:** Term Boggle (create as many science vocabulary words as possible from jumbled letters); Identify the Missing Step (display a scientific process with a step missing); Categories (place the jumbled word cards in the right categories)
- ◆ **ELA:** Literary Terms (either provide a list of literary terms or example sentences using those literary terms, or both). Students can do the following for review: match the terms with the sentences, categorize the sentences according to the literary terms, define the literary terms,

provide their own examples of literary terms, or create a table of juxtaposed terms and determine what sentences might fit in the boxes (see Figure 4.3).

Figure 4.3 Decision Matrix for Literary Terms

	Foreshadow	Dénouement
Climax		
Conflict		

	Foreshadow	Dénouement
Climax	Luke . . .	Alice . . .
Conflict	Wart . . . , Jeff . . .	Senator Cruz . . .

Jeff sliced the dragon open and out came the not-so-beautiful but immensely relieved princess.

Senator Cruz rose to the platform, but before he could testify, the speaker of the house denied him the opportunity with the smash of the gavel.

Alice finally understood what the Cheshire Cat was trying to tell her: If you do not know where you want to go, then anywhere is good enough.

Luke entered the cave and fought Darth Vader and with a swipe of his light saber cut off his head, but when it thudded on the ground, the face looking up at him was his own.

Wart suffered abuse from Kay and Sir Ector in the form of hard labor, verbal slights, and neglect.

♦ **Math:** Fix It (show problems worked out with one error—copied the wrong numbers or operations, misused the properties of equality, did the wrong calculation, or switched digits); Logic Buddies (pair the problems that use the same math operations, or process, for example 5[3x–2] would be paired with [16y–2][3y+5] because both require the use of the distributive property).

♦ **Social Studies:** Timeline (students are given historical events with no dates and they create a timeline, or an incomplete timeline in which they have to fill in the gaps, or a blank timeline in which they fill in the top of the timeline with one topic and the bottom of the timeline with a different topic, e.g., top: scientific breakthroughs, bottom: political breakthroughs. Try having students do a personal timeline of learning on top and significant life events on the bottom).[17]

S T R A T E G Y

Inquiry Learning

Inquiry learning is just that: students asking questions. Some obvious preparations must be made before inquiry learning is employed as a strategy. First, as mentioned earlier, not every lesson can be an inquiry lesson. You do not want students exploring and experimenting with equipment for which they have not had safety training. The safety training would be provided in a "direct" instruction format. Additionally, in mathematics for example, before students can inquire about a mathematical situation, they need to know how to perform the operations. It is unlikely that students will come up with the algebraic theorems of equality on their own; therefore, to save time and frustration, students should be given the theorems and helped to learn them. After that, you can use inquiry to have students devise their own methods for converting inches to millimeters. There is a curriculum program in Texas called CSCOPE[18] that has used a framework called the Five E Learning Cycle.[19] It was primar-

---

[17]One of the most intriguing and creative résumés I have seen is actually a timeline of the individual's work, interests, effort, and preparation, all represented graphically. See for yourself: http://design.spotcoolstuff.com/wp-content/uploads/2010/09/full-infograph-resume.jpg

[18]CSCOPE—This electronic curriculum was based on the research of Dr. John Crain and others. It covers the four core subjects by defining what needs to be taught in Texas through what they call Instructional Focus Documents. It is a collaborative effort of eight of the twenty Regional Service Centers (other states might call these county offices of education, but in Texas there are a gazillion counties, so this limited them to 20). It purports to be aligned vertically and horizontally, contains exemplar lessons, and includes a unit/lesson planning. For more information see www.cscope.us/index.html

[19]Researchers at the University of California, Berkeley, set out to validate theories by Piaget (Learning by Equilibration) and Bruner (Learning by Discovery) and (Learning by Conditioning) by creating the *Science Curriculum Improvement Study* (SCIS) program, a K–6 science program in the early 1970s (see Thier, H., Karplus, R., Lawson, C., Knoll, R., & Montgomery, M. (1970). *Science curriculum improvement study*. Chicago, IL: Rand McNally). In the 80s, the three phases

ily designed for inquiry use in science, but has been applied in other disciplines successfully. The Five E Learning Cycle consists of the following phases: Engage, Explore, Explain, Evaluate, and Enhance. The key to inquiry is that it is the students doing the inquiry, not the teacher. The role of the teacher is to "prime the pump" as necessary to keep the inquiry going and on track, but students are the ones doing the heavy lifting. The teacher's main work in inquiry learning is creating and designing a learning environment that facilitates the discoveries.

TECHNIQUE: Five E's. The first E is **Engage**. The teacher might have to start the inquiry process off with an anticipatory set to get students asking questions, but once students are engaged, the teacher steps back into the facilitator role. For example, the teacher can start by showing a horrific explosion of a car set aflame by the Torch in the second X-Men movie. The car jumps in the air and then spins on its axis horizontally. Then the teacher shows a clip of how the explosion was created using scientific principles (transfer of energy from a rapidly spinning fly wheel to the car).[20] The teacher then shows students the bicycle wheels, the Lazy Susans, swivel chairs, gyroscopes, and other centripetal force devices for the **Explore** phase. Students are given 15 minutes to explore. The **Explain** phase will be the students either writing in their journals or sharing with their partners how spinning objects work and react to different forces. Then in the **Evaluate** phase, students are given the task of traveling from one location to another, balancing on a frame containing two gyroscopes, wait . . . that's riding a bike. Hmm . . . okay, how about this one? Students have to make a top

---

Exploration, Invention, and Discovery were expanded to Engage, Explore, Explain, Evaluate, and Extend in the BSCS science programs. Professor Maryann Coe at Midwestern State University has provided a great explanation of the modern application of the Five E Learning Cycle on her page http://faculty.mwsu.edu/west/maryann.coe/coe/inquire/inquiry retrieved April 30th, 2012.

[20] One of the most engaging learning presentations I have seen is Steve Wolf's Science in the Movies. He came to my little school district and put on several shows for students and workshops for the teachers. Steve is a former stuntman and gives a presentation on how scientific principles are applied in the movies. He demonstrates the states of matter, Newton's Laws, simple machines, and kinetic energy as well as other common scientific principles that students of all ages are learning. To see how you can get him to come to your school, check out his website: www.scienceinthemovies.com

that will spin for the longest amount of time possible using what they have learned. The **Expand** phase consists of students brainstorming about applications for the scientific principles they have learned, such as guidance devices on missiles, Segways®,[21] space vehicles, boats, submarines, hover craft, etc.

---

[21]My mother bought an all-terrain Segway and rides it all over the Arizona desert. Dad takes the dogs, two Great Danes, out for runs every morning with it. Isn't technology marvelous?

Chapter 5

Opportunistic Learners

Opportunistic: Interest in taking advantage of learning opportunities

Why Do Students Need to Be Opportunistic Learners?

I used to own some property in southern Texas and became acquainted with a certain plant called greenbrier.[22] This is a plant that, if left unchecked, will overtake your property in months. It is very hearty and nearly impossible to kill because its roots spread underground and sprouts can appear anywhere. It turns out that the most effective way to deal with this plant is also the most natural way: with a goat. Goats love to eat the plant and actually look for new shoots to pop up.

I would like to compare students to goats in terms of being opportunistic learners. I will also be comparing the learning process to how goats consume and process their food. Pay special note of the bolded words and you will see a remarkable alignment. Goats are hardy quadrupeds that can be found all over the globe. When I was in high school, my mother thought it would be a good idea to get a goat so we could milk her (by "we" she meant me). My mother was always coming up with what we thought were crazy ideas, but

---

[22]Greenbrier is one of the many varieties of *Smilax bona-nox*, of the lily family. It is a tuberous thorny vine that grows as much as three feet in one week and spreads through a system of underground roots that shoot up vines anywhere along the root. Just like Johnson grass, the plant will still be able to grow from any part of the root system left in the ground. It climbs trees and if left unattended can create an almost impenetrable wall of tough, spikey vines.

we'll talk about those later. I need to tell you that goat's milk is very creamy and takes some getting used to. Anyway, we built a comfy pen out of wood and fed her hay and left over veggies. One day we heard the goat bleating in the front of the house (the pen was in the back). We looked in the pen and saw that the goat had eaten through the thin boards on one side of her pen, creating a getaway escape route. She had gotten out so she could have access to a lot of fresh green grass nearby.

This experience got me thinking about goats, though. They are known to eat just about anything, even things that we would not think are edible, such as wood. Goats aren't like cows, which eat only the green grass. Goats will eat the green, the stems, and the roots. Goats will eat the bark off of your trees, the shoes off your feet, and the shirt off your back (especially if it is red—remember "Bill Grogan's Goat?"). You can't tie a goat up with rope; the goat will eat right through it. Speaking of a goat on a rope[23] . . . no, I'd better stay on target. Anyway, goats are pretty indiscriminate about what they eat. Even more than that, as my goat demonstrated, they are opportunistic about what they eat. There is a reason why we only see herds of goats roaming around harsh, inhospitable climates in the Middle East. The goats are successful at finding things to eat that will sustain them in hard times. I should point out that in the next paragraphs, you will receive a biology lesson in the goat gastrointestinal process. But this should come as no surprise because you are already familiar with many of the words that will be used, though you use them in other contexts. Hmm. It is amazing how many words for the digestive process find their way into descriptions of the learning process. For your convenience and added emphasis, I will type the words in bold.

Like goats and their **appetites**, college- and career-ready students need to be opportunistic about what they learn. In order for students to be opportunistic about learning, they, like goats on the lookout for greenbrier shoots, need to be **hungry** for learning opportunities. It is an attitude that creates a constant **thirst** for discovery, exploration, and learning. Please do not stop your students when you find them **grazing** in an encyclopedia or **browsing** in the library. Having an opportunistic learning attitude assumes you are an active learner rather than a passive learner. Now don't get offended, but

---

[23]Josh and Paul were walking through a field and saw a big hole. They wondered how deep it was, so they threw a rock in but didn't hear it hit the ground. They looked around and found a big log, which they dragged over and threw in the hole. Again, they didn't hear a thing, but all of a sudden a goat came running by at an incredible speed and dove down the hole. Still they didn't hear a sound. A bit later a farmer came by looking for his goat. Josh said, "It might be the goat that just ran past and jumped in that big hole back there." "Oh, no," said the farmer, "that can't be . . . my goat is tied to big heavy log."

most teaching that happens in public schools (including in today's student-centered schools) only requires students to be passive learners. Listening is a passive learning activity, like getting sprinkled with water, while reading is an active learning behavior, like grazing on nice green grass (which is different from simply **eating** because it implies that you are covering territory as you eat). A student doesn't need to do anything to listen (and doesn't get much), but students have to engage in many things in order to read, and that makes it more memorable. (Of course, active listening is possible, and if students are really interested, they focus, but in general we do not train students to listen actively. We simply tell them, "Be quiet and pay attention!")

This is where the difference between goats and students makes the comparison difficult, so bear with me. Goats have four stomachs to **digest** the food (stuff) they eat (like other ruminants): the *rumen*, the *reticulum*, the *omasum*, and the *abomasum*. College- and career-ready students must have also the capacity to digest all sorts of knowledge and skills.

The first of the four stomachs in a goat is called the *rumen*. This stomach gathers what goat has **grazed** and then **swallowed**. It acts like a fermentation vat that breaks down the fibers. Periodically, goats will **regurgitate** (cough up) the stuff in the rumen and **chew** it again—this is called **rumination** or **chewing the cud**. College-ready students need to allow information to **ferment** a bit as **enzymes** do their work, and then chew on (**ruminate**) the ideas again later. Rarely will any knowledge produce understanding or long-term memory the first time it is **ingested**.

The second stomach of the goat is called the *reticulum* and looks like a honey-comb. This serves as a **filter** for **undigestable** stuff the goat may have **consumed**. Like goats, students need to filter their knowledge for validity and reliability of sources and **eliminate** the junk. Later we will be talking about validating sources in student research, but for now, a bit of incredulity will go a long way.

The third stomach of the goat is called the *omasum* and is where the water is removed and the major part of the energy nutrients begin to be **absorbed**. As students think, ponder, and meditate on the possibilities of the new knowledge, the ideas are refined, and as a result **fuel** more investigation and thought.

"OK, I know where you are going with this," you say, "and I don't like it!" Calm down— we are talking about the good that the food does to the goat's body (and students' minds), not the **waste** that is discarded. OK?

The final goat stomach is called the *abomasum* (ab-omasum, makes sense). This final stomach is much like our own stomachs and uses caustic acid (HCl) to break down food into **nutrients** the goat's body can **digest**. The nutrients are absorbed in the intestines. College- and career-ready students will be able to take the refined ideas and break them down using critical thinking as if it were acid to eliminate fallacies, falsehoods, and errors and arrive at the **substantive** knowledge. The knowledge is absorbed into the system, and then it can be said of students that they have **"assimilated"** the knowledge.

So there you have it. College- and career-ready students are like goats[24] because they both **consume** opportunistically and have a process to be able to absorb the nutritive substances gained from the browsing or grazing. Also, college- and career-ready students are like goats because they are hardy and only assimilate what does them good. You know what happens with the rest (see Figure 5.1).

Figure 5.1 Digestion and Learning Vocabulary List with Correlation of Goat Digestion and Human Cognition

absorb	appetite	assimilate	chew	chewing the cud	consume
digest	eat	eliminate	enzymes	ingest	ferment
filter	fuel	graze	hunger	nutrients	regurgitate
ruminate	substantive	swallow	thirst	indigestible	waste

Motivate	Obtain	Cogitate	Acquire
Curiosity ♦ Appetite ♦ Substantive	Read ♦ Consume ♦ Eat	Analyze ♦ Reminate ♦ Enzymes ♦ Ferment	Integrate ♦ Digest ♦ Assimilate
Interest ♦ Hunger ♦ Thirst	Browse ♦ Graze	Review/Reflect ♦ Regurgitate ♦ Chew the cud	Understand ♦ Absorb ♦ Nutrients ♦ Fuel
	Listen/Observe ♦ Ingest ♦ Swallow		Refute ♦ Eliminate ♦ Indigestable ♦ Waste

---

[24]If you would like to read more about goats, I found this 4-H site rather helpful www.ansci.cornell.edu/4H/meatgoats/meatgoatfs14.htm

How to Help Students Take Advantage of Learning Opportunities

Learning opportunities abound and are encountered in many diverse situations. The trick is getting students to notice them and then take the time and effort to investigate them. I watched as a magnificent new teacher unfolded the world to students in ways they had never seen. It was a beautiful spring morning in rural Texas. I was going to another campus and noticed a young teacher as a pied piper with her entourage of children following her eagerly. It drew my attention to the situation, and I surreptitiously followed them. It was obvious that these students adored their teacher, not because she was pretty or nice, but because she loved learning and radiated it. I watched as the teacher stopped the class periodically and they huddled around some flower or interesting plant or bug that she found. She asked students why they thought the flower was there, what the bug might eat, and how the plant could move towards the sun. I believe she was a third-grade teacher. I saw her balance on the curb as she walked, and 50 little feet followed. I witnessed her raise her arms gracefully with each step as wings and 50 wings sprouted behind her. The line of students zigzagged and hopped on one foot then the other in perfect cadence with the teacher as they traveled to the gymnasium. No student had to be told to keep up, pay attention, or stay in line because the students were so focused on the teacher and what interesting thing she would find or do. It took only a few minutes extra, but the rewards for the students would last a lifetime. This teacher understood that the best way to get students to be opportunistic learners was to model how to do it herself.

S T R A T E G Y

Immersive Learning

You've heard enough about Benjamin Bloom and his taxonomy, and it is well understood that we must work our way up it in order to more effectively cement knowledge or skills in students' memories. As we discussed earlier, the main reason to use higher-order thinking skills (HOTS) is because students learn better (they remember or retain the knowledge and skills learned) when they are more fully engaged. In terms of Bloom's Taxonomy of the Cognitive Domain, HOTS are at the "application" level or higher. You will recall that HOTS also engage the "Locale" memory system (so named by Caine & Caine, 1991)—instant memory—because they apply situations to learning opportunities. I can think of two instances in which we create HOTS learning systems as parents.

Two examples of immersive learning are when our children are learning how to ride a bike or learning how to swim. Instinctively, in the first case, we set them on the bike and start pushing them around until they get the hang of steering and stopping, and then we give them a big push and they do it on their own.

In the swimming example, we get in the pool with them, and we let them get used to the water. (I don't know of any parents who just throw their children into the pool, but we have all heard of the sink or swim adage.) We show them how to use their arms and feet. We get them used to putting their faces in the water, and then we let them have at it. In both cases, we know they have learned the skill when they have achieved mastery over gravity or water.

Those are examples of HOTS learning systems. I call them systems because all the elements of the environment naturally promote the learning and provide immediate feedback through discovery, practice, and trial and error. The feedback then starts the learning cycle again. Systems are self-sustaining and cyclical.

Within these systems, both the bicycle and the water are essential elements, and they indiscriminately impose consequences for learning—or, for that matter, not learning. This new knowledge then affects the whole cycle. As an illustration of this model, can you imagine trying to teach a child how to ride a bike or swim without using a bike or getting in the water? The water and the bicycle provide the relevance, the urgent need to learn.

TECHNIQUE: Creating learning systems. The true magic or art or science of being a professional educator is having the ability to create learning systems and, in essence, let them loose on students. We should be deliberate in designing our own classroom learning systems. Any true system must have a few elements, as shown in Figure 5.2.

Because I have fond memories of many hours spent in the swimming pool both as a swimmer and a coach, I would like to illustrate this idea of learning systems using a pool as the classroom (see Figure 5.3).

Figure 5.2 Cycle of Learning

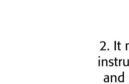
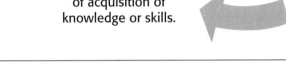

4. It must provide an opportunity for the learners to repeat the step until they get it right (which is the cyclical nature of systems).

1. It needs a personal learning goal.

3. It requires a performance method that demonstrates immediately the level of acquisition of knowledge or skills.

2. It must have direct instruction, modeling, and guided practice in a realistic medium (thanks, Madeline Hunter).

Although learning systems are most typically employed in more hands-on subjects such as the visual or performing arts, physical education, and the laboratory sciences, you can employ them effectively in any classroom.

- For example, a geometry class can set up a rubric for proofs that gives immediate feedback to students regarding their thinking when other students grade them. They then make the corrections and resubmit the proofs.
- In an English class, the process of inner and outer circles establishes a system whereby students can discuss issues and delve more deeply into what they really mean (remember the Socratic Circles we discussed earlier? These are sometime called inner and outer circles). A creative teacher can make these resources available to students and can develop learning systems that automatically promote the kind of learning that engages students in HOTS.

Figure 5.3   Cycle of Learning Swimming Example

4. The swimmer is naturally motivated by the relative success of being able to swim to some degree and not drown and is therefore encouraged to use those skills every time he or she gets in the pool.

1. In the pool, the personal goal is to navigate through the water successfully and not sink.

3. The performance method is the act of attempting to navigate the water. The level of learning is immediately apparent to both the parent and (especially) the struggling and gasping swimmer.

2. Direct instruction, modeling, and guided practice occur when the parent shows the child how to kick and pull the water to provide propulsion.

S T R A T E G Y

Oblique Angles

In the world of geometry, oblique angles are those that are less than 90 degrees. However, when using "oblique" in other ways, it means something that comes at you diagonally, not straight on. The purpose of this strategy is to not deal with the issue in front of us, but the side issues that might surprise us if we took note of them.

Powers of Observation

Students notice all sorts of stuff about teachers, their classrooms, and their friends, but sometimes something might as well be invisible to them because it is so common, or it is so ubiquitous (I find pleasure in using that word, for some reason) that it is under the radar. I think of the *Jungle Book* song by Baloo as he is teaching Mowgli the necessities of life. He talks about turning over a rock and seeing the "fancy ants." Ants are everywhere, and most often we do not notice them because they are under rocks or out of view.

I am reminded of a story about an aspiring young man who wished to be a scientist and learn at the hands of a particular scholar. For weeks, this young man hounded the scholar until finally the professor agreed to take him on as a protégé. The first day, the eager young man arrived at the laboratory of the scholarly professor and asked him to start imparting his wisdom. The old man simply pulled off the shelf a dusty bottle filled with a little fish in formaldehyde. He set the bottle on a stool and said, "Tell me what you see."

Astounded at the easiness of the task, the young man responded, "This is nothing more than a fish in a bottle."

The old man shook his head wearily and said, "Keep looking." And then he walked out of the room.

This pattern was repeated for the next few days as the young man's frustration grew. After a week of this, the young man could not take it any longer. He decided he was going to talk to the professor in his office and inform him that he would be seeking another mentor. On the way, the young man struggled to reconcile the glowing praise that his comrades and the other professors had shared about this professor. What was he supposed to learn from simply looking at a fish in a bottle?

It occurred to the young man that he didn't even know what kind of fish he was complaining about. "That won't do," he thought. "To effectively complain, I need to at least know what kind of fish it is!"

So instead of going to the old professor's office, he went to the lab again, took down the old bottle, and started looking for identifying marks on the fish. He pulled down some books on fish and began the process of identifying this little fish. He looked closely at the scale patterns, the fin placement, and the other markings. He had to pull more reference books off the shelves, still attempting to identify this little fish. The more he looked at this fish, the more he found that was unusual. After an hour, surrounded by reference books, drawings, and other fish in bottles, the young man was still engrossed in the details of this little fish.

When the old professor came to look in on his pupil, he simply grinned, nodded his head, and matter-of-factly stated, "You are making progress."

Chapter 6

Flexible Learners

Flexibility: Ability and desire to cope with frustration and ambiguity

Why Do Students Need to Be Flexible Learners?

A while ago, I did an experiment with adult educators. I purposely gave very vague instructions on how to arrange groups. The goal was for each educator to participate in three different groups. I told them that the composition of each group had to be different. Their task was to get four different signatures for each of three groups listed on their worksheet. Everyone got one set of signatures right away. Getting the next set of signatures was more difficult because it had to be with different people. Some of the adults were willing to work it out, even using trial and error. Others would get to a point and realize that they did not understand what to do, and then would ask questions. A few began getting upset at the lack of directions and refused to try. I was hoping that the adults would be able to work together to negotiate the groups, but the project failed entirely. One adult asked me, "Why didn't you just ask us to count off by numbers and be done with it?" The reason I did not do this was that this little experiment informed me of the flexibility of thinking of the group and helped me to customize the instruction I would be giving them.

From this simple example, we can infer that our students probably belong in one of these three groups: being comfortable with uncertainty, being uncomfortable with uncertainty, and being irritated with uncertainty. In a 2011 study on student motivation, Kyndt, Dochy, Struyven, & Cascallar discovered that when students were given more autonomy, even though the amount of information or the level of uncertainty was the same, students perceived that there was less uncertainty and were more apt to adopt a deep approach to learning rather than a superficial one. A certain amount of uncertainty cannot be avoided. Uncertainty is messy, it is disorganized, it is unstructured, and it is organic. When doubt exists and the answer or path is not known beforehand, that is the essence of uncertainty. Apparently, according to the research, if students have to wait around for teachers to tell them what to do, the anxiety about uncertainty is raised, and students tend to go through the motions of learning as a result. But when students are internally motivated to learn, they are better able to cope with uncertainty, and they show resiliency in the face of not knowing precisely what to do next.

One of the main goals of the CCSS is to prepare learners to be college- and career-ready by helping them deal with uncertainty and by helping them feel comfortable in postulating, guessing, hypothesizing, conjecturing, and testing their theories without knowing the answers and without knowing if there even is an answer. To our shame in public education, we have socialized students into believing that there is always a right answer and that the teacher is the guardian of that answer. We have misinformed students to such an extent that they believe that not being certain is a bad thing. As a result, few students are willing to take a risk and demonstrate their vulnerability. As I described earlier, the summer I spent with 30 Ford PAS students from inner-city schools in San Antonio showed me that it in six weeks, this attitude can be turned around. Before I discuss how to do this, I want to make sure we understand what I am trying to communicate.

Helping students feel at ease with ambiguity does not mean that students remain blithely ignorant of the details. It means helping students deal effectively with an ambiguous situation and providing a means to clarify the situation. It means helping students confront uncertainty by identifying what is certain. It means helping students minimize the risks of getting the wrong answer and feel confident that instead of having to choose the correct answer, they can choose the best answer and support their decision. The purpose of this chapter is to provide a few ideas on how to help students develop strategies for dealing with uncertainty, ambiguity, and frustration.

Teachers need to inject a little uncertainty into their lessons every day because it engages students at the "analysis and above" levels commonly known as higher-order thinking skills (HOTS). This uncertainty forces students to evaluate what they know and do not know and to make decisions about it. Let's borrow an example from Steven R. Covey (1989), where he gives his audience a seemingly impossible task. He first fills a bucket with sand and asks an audience member to put all of the pebbles and larger rocks in the bucket. After several unsuccessful attempts, the participant gives up. Then Dr. Covey gives the participant a bucketful of rocks and tells the person to put in the pebbles and then the sand and water. Amazingly, it all fits. The message of prioritization provided by Dr. Covey's demonstration is not lost, but in this scenario, I am more interested in another message: when faced with the unknown, the improbable, or the impossible, a solution is discoverable if you have a strategy.

Thinking about sand and water, a math teacher could demonstrate the following problem:

"Here we have a 100 ml beaker that is filled with sand and weighs 16 ounces. What is the volume of the sand?

"100 millimeters!" the class responds.

"That is easy, right? Now let's magnify what we see in the beaker of sand."

The teacher holds up a beaker full of medium-sized rocks and asks, "If this represents the sand at high magnification, what do you notice about the volume?"

"There are gaps between the rocks."

"That is correct. Talk to your neighbor and come up with a way that you could you find the real volume of the sand. Discuss what other materials you would need and what math you would need to use to find the solution. You have five minutes."

This problem challenges students to think about what they know about volume and what assumptions they have made about the sand, mathematically and scientifically. Depending on students' age, various interesting activities can be done to investigate how the true volume of the sand can be measured.

In reality, the uncertainty principle is an inextricable part of math, statistics, and especially science, and as a matter of fact, it is accepted that any research involves a certain amount of uncertainty. There is no such thing as an exact science, so why would teaching and learning be any different? Students who feel confident in the face of uncertainty are better prepared to look at all the possibilities before choosing the best answer. These students are less concerned about being told what to know and are more concerned with understanding why it should be known and how to know it.

How to Help Students Cope with Frustration and Ambiguity

Robotics competitions are full of frustration and ambiguity. Teams from all over the United States compete in the U.S. FIRST Robotics Competition.[25] Last year it was held in St. Louis, Missouri. Each year, student teams are given a different task for their robots to complete. For the 2012 competition, the task was collecting basketballs and tossing them through the hoops. Students had to construct a robot that was no taller than seven feet and no wider than three feet. The robot had to be able to move by radio control and have mechanisms that could pick up a basketball and toss it through hoops of three different heights. And the robot had only two minutes and 15 seconds to do it. The robot had to follow specific rules and got fouls and penalties for breaking those rules.

The robotics team had to build the robot from scratch. With these parameters, the students designed a robot. They had to determine how the robot would move, what method would be utilized to retrieve balls, and how they would get the robot to shoot them. They were given no designs, no direction, and no limits other than the size limits. They made their conceptual drawings and then had to find out if the concept would work. They were allowed to make mini robots to test their theories, or they could construct the individual mechanisms for testing. Once they completed all the testing, then they built the full robot and did more testing.

By the time a team has made it to the national competition, they have already competed in local and regional ones, and most of the technology glitches have been worked out so they can focus more on strategies for dealing with the other competing robots and perfecting their robot-driving skills.

When I went to our local region with our fledgling team of robotics students for a simple Lego robotics competition, it was an eye-opening experience. Because this was our first time, my students were uncertain what the competition would be like. We also had a technical glitch, so the robot was still untested because certain parts of the program had to be rewritten due to the battery falling out when students arrived. During the competition, our robotics team discovered that there was a strategy of dealing with other robots that somehow our team had not considered. Unfortunately, because of this surprise and first-time jitters, our team did not perform well (we didn't even get past the first round).

---

[25]FIRST Robotic Competitions began in 1992 in New Hampshire and have grown to be a national competition involving almost 250,000 students. You might be interested to see video footage of past competitions at www.usfirst.org.

In designing the robots, the biggest concern is the ability to perform the main functions. There are no guidelines, construction manuals, or directions on how to make your robot pick up a basketball and throw it, or in our case follow a printed line, grab thimbles, and drop them. This is uncertainty at its maximum. There are obvious ways to minimize the uncertainty: create detailed plans before you build the robot, test the parts independently before you assemble the robot, or build a smaller prototype robot and test it out before you build the big one. In the case of the St. Louis Competition, the robotics teams had access to detailed dimensions and operations of the court, as well as actual videos of the court. These are important aids to reducing the ambiguity and uncertainty produced by these competitions. In the case of the smaller competition in which we participated, the instructions were entirely written and did not provide an easy way of conceptualizing what would really happen. Our students did the best they could, but considerable frustration could have been eliminated with a few simple photographs.

With that in mind, teachers need to be careful to identify the aims of any learning activity designed to help students deal with ambiguity, uncertainty, and frustration. There is nothing more frustrating to students than a teacher, who in the name of "building character" in students, proposes that students engage in learning activities that have not been well thought out and prepared. In a student's mind, there is not much difference between a "complete waste of time" and "I want to see how you perform under stress." Inserting unknowns should be done on purpose and sparingly. Providing some answers or concreteness is primarily to help students focus on what is most important to learn rather than to have students figure out what to do. The idea of inquiry in boosting learning is best applied in small doses. Create learning environments—or what I call islands or bubbles of learning—within the limits of which students do not know the answers and must investigate and explore. Students must also be given a time limit and a rubric to gauge successful completion of the inquiry; otherwise the inquiry could take too much time and accomplish too little.

This reminds me of a frustrating video game that we purchased for my son a few years ago. As it turns out, there is a series of video games called the Elder Scrolls[26] that came out a few years ago, and my one and only experience

---

[26]Bethesda Softworks released the first of the Elder Scroll series role play games in 1994 as an MSDOS game. Morrowind was marketed as an Xbox game in May of 2003 and is the third in the series. Two sequels follow Morrowind: Oblivion and Skyrim. Check Morrowind out at www.elderscrolls.com/morrowind. Be careful, however; if the sequels are like Morrowind, be prepared to spend lots of time in the interesting worlds. They can become quite addictive or so I am told. I wouldn't know by experience of course. The MacIntosh Myst series of games was a precursor to this game; it is just as engaging, but the actions and physical awareness is much more limited.

with it began with a game called Morrowind. It is a role-playing game that draws you in by not providing any information to start. The game begins by asking you what type of person you wish to be and what race. That is all you get. There is no help, no instructions, no idea of what you are to accomplish. Your new character has to investigate, observe, and ask the residents of the game a lot of questions. As you explore the Morrowind virtual world, you discover a plot and what might be your role. This is an example of pure inquiry, but Morrowind is not a game that can be completed in days, weeks, or even months of playing. I logged many hours, and I still didn't come close to reaching the end. Anyway, the whole game is about finding out what you are about, and that is what inquiry is: going into a situation and not knowing what you will bring out. It takes some planning and some teacher trust to allow students to engage in inquiry learning, but the results are good for students and good for learning. Some other interesting developments are occurring in interactive worlds such as Google's Lively, Eduism for education, and Secondlife.

Another strategy is project-based learning, which is what the robotics programs really are. Given a problem, you have to come up with a solution or a product. Edutopia.org is a website that specializes in project-based design and contains many examples of projects performed by students and how to design them effectively. Unsurprisingly, it was created by George Lucas, who figured that there had to be a better way to teach students than the way he was taught in public schools.[27] Fortunately, the push for college- and career-readiness inherent in the CCSS is perfectly in sync with George Lucas's vision of useful education. There is a better way for students to learn, and at the heart of that improvement must be the students' active, willing, and even eager engagement in the learning process. When students are able to handle frustration and ambiguity, they are well on their way to becoming college- and career-ready. Following are some active learning strategies and techniques that will help students seek opportunities to learn.

---

[27]The George Lucas Education Foundation promotes evidence-based strategies that improve student learning in innovative and replicable ways. They emphasize project-based learning and technology integration in schools. Check them out at www.edutopia.org, and while you are there, you can check me out—I am one of their featured bloggers.

STRATEGY

Prime the Pump. Here's the Main Idea— You Work Out the Details

The unique roles of teacher and student in modern schools pose a conundrum. A teacher has knowledge and experience, and students need that. The problem is that a teacher cannot just give knowledge and skills to students. If he does, then students will not, and for the most part cannot, take advantage of them. In essence, the knowledge and skills offered will be wasted. In order for students to be able to really acquire, assimilate, and integrate the knowledge and skills, students must seek knowledge and skills for themselves and find them on their own terms. They must reinvent the wheel in order to appreciate it and improve on it. The hardest part of this process for students is getting started. It is at this juncture that the best role of the teacher is to prime the pump and then get out of the way.

TECHNIQUE: Magic wand. Sometimes students are inhibited by reality and do not know where to begin in terms of projects. At these times, a teacher can change the situation by giving them a magic wand that can ignore reality. This wand can be selective or all-inclusive. You can creatively limit the power of the wand to drive the thinking in productive directions. For an example of a selective wand, you set up a learning scenario in which students must communicate with martians, and the wand allows only the martians to understand the students, but they still cannot understand the martian speech. "How can you get around this problem and still communicate effectively with the martians?"

TECHNIQUE: Rubrics. Simply writing down what students are to accomplish helps refine the standards of performance and diminish the ambiguity. When students know what kind and quality of product they must produce, they have a better idea of where to direct their search for learning opportunities.

The Future Is Uncertain

My son Gideon's favorite animated movie for a while was *Meet the Robinsons*.[28] Aside from having catchy music, the movie is appealing because the theme song has a good message, "The future is alive . . ." The main character, Robinson, learns that the key to a happy life is to "keep moving forward." For students, the future is nebulous because the only thing they can judge it by is the present. But they can keep moving forward. The value of projecting current behaviors into the future (trend analysis) gives students a coping mechanism for dealing with the uncertainty of the future.

TECHNIQUE: Plan ten years in the future. The perfect tool for this technique is the spreadsheet. Mathematics teachers can capitalize on the "Fill Series" command to help students create linear projections of the future. In the spreadsheet, students type in a beginning number, then highlight that number and nine cells below it. Once highlighted, students can either use the menu or shortcuts to define the "Step" or gap between numbers (i.e., for 1, 2, 3 . . . the Step would be 1. For 2, 4, 6 . . . the Step would be 2, and so on . . .). Having chosen "1" as the initial number, if the Step is 2, then the resulting numbers will be 1, 3, 5, 7 . . .

To perform geometric or exponential projections, students will need to know how to create and copy corresponding formulas into cells. The teacher can provide concrete examples of growth models: bacteria reproduction, simple vs. compound interest, acceleration of free falling objects, etc. Students can begin comparing linear growth to geometric or exponential growth and predict the outcome after ten years. Students can represent the growth graphically (and creatively) in numerous ways.

Another useful but slightly more advanced command is the "Goal Seek" command. Given a formula, students can select a target value that is derived from different elements in the formula. The program will automatically

---

[28] A 2007 Disney animated movie about an orphaned boy named Lewis, who is brought into his future to resolve an evil plot and in the process meets his future family and learns a few things about himself. See http://disneydvd.disney.go.com/meet-the-robinsons.html

adjust those elements to arrive at the sought after goal. This is particularly useful in situations where changing one variable also affects the other variable. "Goal Seek" is a balancing act that is much better suited for the computer to figure out. This is one of those cases in which it is better to give students the tool rather than have them try to figure it out on their own. With the "Goal Seek" tool, students will be able to engage in predicting the future based on changing one variable in the equation.

SECTION II
CONCLUSION

College- and Career-Ready Learners Feel a Sense of Urgency

What you believe as a teacher is the reality of your instruction. Everything you do as a teacher stems from what you value most. Students notice this, but have you noticed how much of an influence you, as a teacher, have on the way students feel about learning in your classroom? Your interests, your curiosity, and your skills can all find reflections in the eyes of your students. You are the model that your students aspire to become.

We've all had days when we are on fire, students are excited, and everything seems to happen just the way we planned. Why can't we have those days every day? There are a multitude of reasons, but most of them are either related to or directly linked with what we as teachers do. Yes, there are always student issues, but we can anticipate those and compensate for them. So if the teacher controls the mood and energy of the class, what feeling should you have to prepare students to be college- and career-ready when they leave your classroom? May I suggest a sense of urgency? (But not the restroom kind.)

To get an idea of what urgency feels like, let's look at the story about the would-be student of a great teacher: The student pressed the teacher to tell him what he must do to gain great knowledge. After much badgering, the teacher finally told the pupil to meet him at the beach the next morning so he could answer his question.

The next day, they met on the beach. The teacher walked into the water and motioned for the student to follow. When the student got close, the teacher grabbed him and pushed his head underwater, holding it there for a while. The student struggled, first because of his surprise and then because he needed air. Finally the teacher let the student up, gasping for breath. The teacher asked the student, "While you were underwater, what did you want more than anything else?" "Breath!" was the ragged reply. The teacher explained, "If you want great knowledge, then you must want it as badly as you wanted to breathe."

Do you have that sense of urgency in front of your students? Can you imagine getting your students to feel that level of urgency? It is possible if we establish a learning environment that promotes it. The very first factor is that we have to be on fire before we will kindle any fire in our students. We set the mood with our expressions, the way we walk, and the tone of our voices. We have to ask ourselves each class, "Am I urgent enough to inspire students to want to learn?"

Often the kind of urgency we want in our students is intrinsic to the learning activity itself. Drawing out this powerful urgency means that our learning tasks have to be important and must require immediate attention. First, we must provide a reason to learn (which is analogous to sticking the student's head underwater). Second, we have to establish a need in our students to learn now (like a person whose head is underwater and needs to breathe). Here are my ideas for learning systems that promote urgency (see Figure II.4).

In order for learning activities to be most effective, you have to design them to be part of a learning system in which all the parts work together. If the teacher's behavior demonstrates a sense of urgency, students' behavior will most likely follow suit. Urgency is the spark of energy students need to engage in the difficult task of acquiring knowledge and skills. If applied correctly, the process of teaching and learning is efficient and fun. So when students enter your classroom, you want them to want to feel a sense of urgency. They need to want to learn what you have prepared as badly as they want to breathe.

In this section, we have discussed developing an inquisitive nature in each student, helping students to take advantage of learning opportunities, and strategies that will help students deal effectively with uncertainty and ambiguity. Combine all of that with an intense sense of urgency, meaning they have important things to learn right away, and students will be well on their way to becoming college- and career-ready.

Figure II.4 Learning Environments that Promote Urgency

Provide a Reason to Learn: Make It Relevant

- Establish realistic products the students will create as a result of the desired learning.
- Bring in an expert who can give the students real-life problems they need to solve using the desired knowledge.
- Make connections with the other subjects the students are learning about.

Establish a Need to Do It Now — Make It Time Bound

- Set up time limits and follow up with consequences for not meeting them.
- Organize races and contests. (Check out an example of a math contest called Subtraction War, from Teachers.net.)
- Help students set their own goals and timelines.

Make It Personal — Measure and Celebrate Success

- Allow students to choose among different methods, not just levels of difficulty or depth.
- Give students an opportunity to present or publish their work outside of class.
- Prepare and administer pretests to which students can compare how much they have learned.

Building Resiliency

The Hard Work and Exhilaration of Learning Builds Resiliency

"Just two hundred more yards!" Flip, push off, breathe. Right, left, right, breathe. Left, right, left, breathe.

"Remember, long stroke, all the way forward and all the way back, deep." I can't get enough breath. Flip, push off, breathe . . . breathe again.

"You can do it, Ben!" My arms are complaining; the ache goes down to the fingertips.

"Only one hundred fifty left! Don't slow down." Kick more. Keep the rhythm: stroke, kick, stroke, kick, stroke, kick, breathe, repeat . . . Flip, push off, breathe . . . big breath.

"Only fifty left. Pick it up! Pull harder, all the way forward and all the way back." Have to breathe every stroke. Gasp. Pulse is pounding, adrenaline kicks in . . . swimming faster, harder.

"Almost there!" Must keep swinging the arms even though they feel like lead: right, left, right . . .

"Done!" Rest, check pulse, float. Exhilaration!

I met a goal to swim a mile freestyle without stopping last summer. Some might call me crazy, though others in the pool went much farther and faster than I did. It was hard work that required everything I had in order to complete it. I knew I could do it, but I had not done it since I was in college thirty years ago. I did it because I knew it would be a milestone for me to get further in shape. I didn't worry about how long it took me; speed would come later. I met my goal to swim a thousand six hundred and fifty yards freestyle without stopping, even though there were no cheering crowds or gold medals. Still, I knew I had accomplished a tremendous feat for me, and that made all the difference. My motivation was internal and self-perpetuating. In this chapter we will be talking about motivation and factors that contribute to developing it.

Let me remind you and all of your students that learning is hard work, just like swimming a mile without stopping. Any coach can tell you that growth only comes when you stretch further than you think you can and practice more than you think you can endure. When you read deeper, think longer, and create more enthusiastically, that is when the learning really happens.

Then, when you help students admire their work, it is exhilarating for them to know that they have accomplished a challenging and difficult goal. More likely than not, no one will know how much they have learned, but you will know and they will know. There will be no cheering crowds and no fame or fortune. Nevertheless, because you show your students by pretesting and post testing how much they have progressed, they will feel satisfied, complete . . . ready for more. Their motivation to learn more will be fueled just because they completed their challenging learning goal. Surprisingly, the hard work has not scared them off and their resolve and determination to succeed has not diminished. The eagerness for the next learning adventure wells up within them as they reach out for new knowledge and skills. This is when learning is fun!

Each student needs and deserves his or her own internal motivation to learn. In order for this to blossom within the students, some simple things need to happen. Teachers need to create an atmosphere of belonging to a high-performance learning team—learning is the goal and every learning activity (adventure) is designed to bring the students closer to that goal.

I have been privileged to witness teachers who have done these very things for their students, and I thank them for instilling this lifelong learning drive and thirst for knowledge in me. In this section, I will encourage you to teach students how to seek after and accept critical feedback, adjust to that feedback, face daunting tasks like swimming a mile, and develop the resiliency necessary to be active, college- and career-ready learners (see Figure III.1).

Figure III.1 Eight Things Students Need in Order to Learn

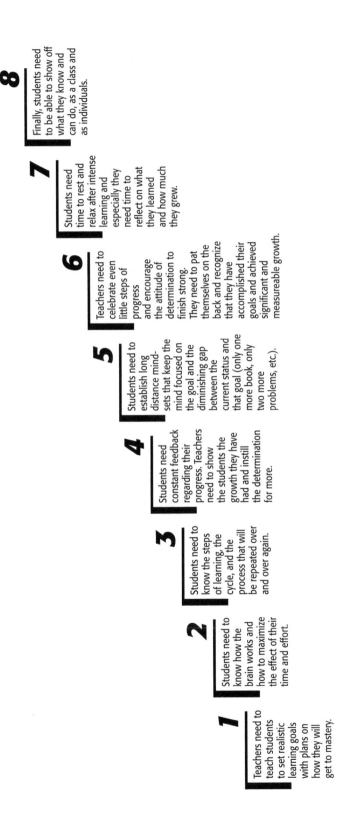

1 Teachers need to teach students to set realistic learning goals with plans on how they will get to mastery.

2 Students need to know how the brain works and how to maximize the effect of their time and effort.

3 Students need to know the steps of learning, the cycle, and the process that will be repeated over and over again.

4 Students need constant feedback regarding their progress. Teachers need to show the students the growth they have had and instill the determination for more.

5 Students need to establish long distance mind-sets that keep the mind focused on the goal and the diminishing gap between the current status and that goal (only one more book, only two more problems, etc.).

6 Teachers need to celebrate even little steps of progress and encourage the attitude of determination to finish strong. They need to pat themselves on the back and recognize that they have accomplished their goals and achieved significant and measureable growth.

7 Students need time to rest and relax after intense learning and especially they need time to reflect on what they learned and how much they grew.

8 Finally, students need to be able to show off what they know and can do, as a class and as individuals.

Chapter 7

Willingness to Accept Critical Feedback

Accepting critical feedback:
Eagerness to find ways to improve

Why Do Students Need to Be Able to Accept Critical Feedback?

How do you help students accept and even seek critical feedback in today's society of everyone is a winner? The entitlement attitude of "showing up gets me a trophy" is not going to work in the real world. So how do you get students to first of all accept critical feedback and secondly, want it? Before I answer that question, it is important to make sure we are on the same page in terms of what critical feedback means. Critical feedback is what happens when the results are compared to the expectations. Critical feedback implies that the goals were not met, but the most important part of that feedback is what was wrong and how to fix it. Students deserve to know when they did not meet the standards, what they got wrong, and how they can fix the problem. Now this is where some educators start cringing. I said "problem" and "wrong" in the same sentence. We are not supposed to say such mean words. We must use words such as "areas of enhancement," not student problems. Believe it or not, most students appreciate it when they are told that their performance could have been better and are given specific ways that they can improve it.

Perfection is unattainable in this life. Everyone can do better at everything. Teachers do no favor to a student by withholding negative feedback. This is not to say once a student has reached mastery that you keep criticizing, but use the Big Mac approach (a criticism sandwiched between two compliments) and it is easier to swallow. Students deserve to know the good and the bad (yes I said bad) and even the ugly.[29] How are they supposed to know how to improve unless they are tested against a standard and receive continual feedback? After all, it is all about learning, right?

Another thing to consider is our learning plan. For example, when a student is given a learning assignment to turn in, is it really a "learning" assignment if they have only one chance at meeting the mastery level standard? How are they supposed to show that they have "learned" if they only get to do it once? Here is a suggestion. When a student submits a substandard piece of work, rather than assign a grade immediately, we can provide personalized, individual feedback to that student, including suggestions for improvement, and give it back to the student for revision!

Is there a limit to the number of times this can be done to help a student overcome a particular learning obstacle? Some students might be able to do it right the first time, while others need several revisions. Typically we see this kind of opportunity in English and social studies classes. It's called a "rough draft." Why not do the same in math and science? After all, if the student eventually gets the concept, isn't that what counts? The thing I like about the concept of assessing to provide feedback for improved performance the next time around is that no student is left out—not even the quiet, no-problem kids.

Using assessments as a learning tool is not necessarily a new topic. It is rare, but the concept has been around a while. I would like to revisit it with a personal analogy. I took the Cisco Networking Class one summer, and we completed a whole semester of a high school course in one week.[30] We spent

---

[29]Clint Eastwood's 1966 film, *The Good, the Bad and the Ugly*, has a special place in my heart. My wife and I had just returned from our honeymoon, and were settling in our new place. We decided that we wanted to watch the video of our wedding reception. We pulled out the videocassette that a friend had videotaped for us and sat down to enjoy. Lo and behold, instead, we saw a recording of Clint Eastwood's *The Good, the Bad, and the Ugly*. We did find the real tape eventually; luckily it had not been recorded over, but it gave us a scare, and a laugh.

[30]Cisco Inc. has a marvelous program, the Cisco Networking Academy, of which schools can take advantage to help students become certified Cisco Networking Technicians. In order to establish a training facility on your campus, a teacher must attend the training first and become certified. Then for a minimum amount of money, the school can purchase the necessary laboratory equipment (routers, switches, and hubs) on which students can practice. Established correctly in a campus, students attending such a lab will be able to have their initial networking certification already completed before going to a trade school or college. For more information, see www.cisco.com/web/learning/netacad/index.html

two hours listening to a lecture of the key points and then we took a test. In order to continue in the program, we had to pass the test with an 85%. Talk about high stakes!

When I was taking the tests, I noticed something. Since we had studied the chapter the night before (supposedly), and since we had just gone over the material, you would think the tests would have been easy, but some of the questions were designed to trick us into selecting the wrong answer. So even though I was well versed in the material and it was fresh in my mind, I never aced any of the tests. (Grrr.) I passed them—most reasonably well and some just barely—but it was frustrating to not do perfectly. The fact that others were struggling too helped assuage my pride, but the one student in the class who got 100% got open congratulations from all of us and . . . at least from me, he got a silent, "I'll catch you yet!"

Anyway, this got me thinking. If we want to test a student's knowledge, shouldn't we just straight out ask the question? Is it necessary to throw in distracters, misleading answers, and ones that are close to the right answer but not quite? Is that fair?

Hold that thought. I remember taking the "Assessment Design" class in college and saying to myself, "What teacher is going to have time to make all of these test questions and design a scientific pretest and posttest for every unit?" I have since discovered the answer to that question. I know that I did not make or take the time to make such elaborate quizzes or tests, and from my personal experience, neither do many other teachers. Another question then: If valid assessment is so important, how do you do this? Before I answer that, let's go back to my other thought.

Distracters, misleading answers, and trick questions are important for establishing level of difficulty; we can't get rid of them! Since we have to differentiate our instruction, why not our tests too? The same students who have different learning needs are the same ones taking the tests. Another reason is that there are two types of tests, summative and formative. One of the safety nets of my Cisco class was that our instructor gave us three chances to take the test. After taking each test, we could look at the right answers and figure out what we did wrong and then take the test again. This is the main characteristic of formative tests—a chance to take it again. But when I go back and figure out how I blew the question, I actually learn better. It sticks in my brain better!

Back in my college Assessment Design class, I learned that each test needs to have some easy questions, some challenging questions, and some hard questions. A sophisticated teacher will assign different point values for each. A more sophisticated teacher will make sure that each question is also aligned with a state standard (but that is a conversation for another day). Anyway, the struggling student will most likely get the easy questions, while the advanced student will be challenged with the hard ones. Both feel that the test has made them stretch, and both can feel success in the questions answered correctly.

How can we find time for this? The way to find time is simple (unless you teach in a small school where you are the only teacher and are willing to give up your summer vacation to redo all of your tests by mining the textbooks and the Internet). You work with your teacher peers and come up with the tests (pre and post) together. You share ideas, and you design a better mouse trap . . . I mean you design a better test, as a group. Now if you consider the sophistication I've mentioned, you all will be able to gather valuable student information that helps you compare teaching performance . . . and predict student performance on state testing. Some other time-saving tools are question item banks, scanners, and online test-taking tools. If made together, the test will be a better product, and it will be more useful, more productive, and less time-consuming for the teacher.

We can't expect students to spend several hours studying each night and be excited about taking tricky tests, but we can challenge them with well-designed, differentiated, and useful assessments so they can learn and experience successes from meeting challenges. That will excite them.

How to Give Formative Assessments to Help Students Accept Critical Feedback

I've been bowling recently, as perhaps have some of you. There are some unusual things about bowling you can directly apply to improving classroom learning, so let's go bowling for a minute.

Imagine you are at a bowling alley. You brought your own beautiful bowling ball, and you are wearing your stylishly-patterned bowling shoes. As soon as you step up to the lane, however, someone ties a blindfold over your eyes so you can't see a thing. Undaunted, you launch your ball down the lane, and you hear the solid crash of a ball against pins. But there is so much noise in the building that you can't tell whether it was your ball or someone else's. You wonder, "Did I get a strike, or was it a gutter ball?"

How long do you think you would continue to bowl if you could not see what you were aiming at, and you never knew if you even hit a pin? I know I wouldn't last very long. It would be pointless.

The most enjoyable thing about bowling is seeing how you did after each throw. You are in charge of your own performance, and you get to see the results as a natural consequence. As with any endeavor, if you do it enough, you can often get pretty good at it, which is even more fun. Bowling is one of many learning systems that give participants intrinsic feedback to improve, and feedback is the most important element of formative assessment.

Education, like bowling, is most fun and effective when the learner is in charge of his own improvement. He sees the goal, gives his best shot at meeting it, gets feedback to make corrections, and then tries again. If the bowler does not knock down all ten pins on the first roll, he gets another chance to knock down the ones still standing.

The bowler is dependent on being able to see what happens when the ball he has just released strikes the pins. The next time he rolls the ball, he applies what he learned from the first roll to do it better. If it works, great! He's achieved success. If it doesn't, then it is not failure. He simply tries again. Everyone is a lousy bowler the first go-around. It's the repetition that makes us better. So why do we expect our students to knock down all ten content pins the first time they pick up the ball?

STRATEGY

Peer Review

This strategy does not just mean having students exchange papers to grade. In order for it to work, you first must trust students be serious on how they grade. Most students would much rather be graded by the teacher, but that is not the point of this exercise. The point of the exercise is that the grader will have to critique another peer's paper and provide suggestions on how to improve it. Just as a teacher learns much more about a subject in the preparation for teaching than do the students, the peer evaluator will learn a tremendous amount by evaluating another student's work. The other thing that the teacher must do is to provide a bit of training on how this should be done. A simple framework form, like the one that follows in Figure 7.1, will help students focus on providing effective critiques. The next thing that the teacher must make available is a detailed rubric of the assignment (see Figure 7.2). Notice the plus, minus, and plus in the heading. This is to remind students to first look for a positive, then provide one negative, then end with a positive.

Figure 7.1   Technique: Peer Review Checklist

Writing Guides	1–5	Notes for Peer Review (+, –, +)
Genre		
Style		
Tone		
Mechanics		
Spelling		
Grammar		
Punctuation		
Organization		
Thesis statement		
Introductory paragraph		
Body		
Conclusion		
Detail		
Facts		
Opinion		
Evidence		
Examples		
Authority		
Sources		
References		
Validity		

Figure 7.2   Technique: Peer Review Rubric

Needs Work	Nearly There	Adequate
Genre		
Writing style may be evident. Too much or too little description.	Writing style is inconsistent. Ideas may be disjointed. Description too detailed.	Writing style is easy to read and ideas are easy to follow. Not too descriptive.
Too much tone or not enough tone.	The tone is over the top in some instances.	The tone is appropriate for the genre. Not overbearing or caustic. Generally happy.

Figure 7.2 Technique: Peer Review Rubric (*continued*)

Needs Work	Nearly There	Adequate
Mechanics		
Several spelling errors	Few spelling errors	No spelling errors
Several grammar errors	Few grammatical Errors	No grammatical errors.
Punctuation is an obstacle to understanding, or missing.	Punctuation causes confusion in some cases.	Punctuation aids comprehension and ease of reading.
Organization		
Thesis statement missing or not identifiable.	Thesis is identifiable but not clear.	Clearly stated thesis.
Introductory paragraph is missing or incomplete.	Introduces the main ideas but not creatively.	Introduction is interesting and engaging.
Some of the body supports the thesis statement	Most of the body supports the thesis statement	Body supports the thesis statement.
Conclusion reviews some of the thesis statement or is incomplete.	Most of the thesis statement is reviewed in the conclusion.	The thesis points are reviewed in the conclusion.
Detail		
Some of the facts are faulty or incorrect.	Few of the facts appear faulty.	Data appears to be factual.
Some opinion is given the same status as fact.	Most opinion is treated with caution.	Opinion is treated with caution.
Some statements are supported by evidence and examples.	Most statements supported by evidence and examples.	Statements are supported by evidence and examples.
Authority		
Some references are listed and cited.	Most references are listed and cited.	References are listed and cited.
Some sources for references are valid and reliable.	Most sources for references are valid are reliable.	The sources for the references are valid and reliable.

Chapter 8

Willingness to Adjust Based on Feedback

Willing to adjust learning:
Capacity to alter course mid-stream

Why Do Students Need to Be Willing to Adjust Their Learning?

As we learned earlier, when you bowl, you get to see where the ball goes and what the result is, strike or spare. In basketball, you see the ball's arc and hear the swish, or else you have to go for the rebound. In softball, while swinging the bat you hear the crack and see the ball zooming away, or you hear the smack of the catcher's mitt. Each of these is an example of immediate feedback that informs the athletes and allows them to improve on the next turn. The same could be said of any sport that requires aiming. Having the opportunity to shoot more than once serves to improve the score by using what was learned from previous shots. But interestingly enough, being able to try again and strive for this very improvement is the sole exhilaration and motivation for participating in the sport in the first place. How interesting would bowling be if the bowling ball were only rolled down the alley once? What would be the draw with baseball if the pitcher were only allowed one pitch for each batter? There are some obvious connections to education here. Far too often in education, we do not provide immediate feedback to students, and by failing to do so, in a single stroke, we eliminate the sole exhilaration and motivation for learning in the first place.

Flexibility Is Fomented by Feedback—True Formative Assessment

Not only does my example show immediate feedback, but it is also shows formative assessment. (How is that for awesome alliteration? FFF) By "formative" I mean "having the capacity to form, or being capable of altering the form of something malleable." That sounds amazingly similar to what we perceive that educators do in general. We change a student from being stupid to smart, unintelligent to intelligent, uninformed to informed, unskillful to skillful, ignorant to knowledgeable, and so on. If we follow this reasoning, then as teachers we are doing all the work and should get all the credit, right? Hang on there. Doesn't this sound awfully boastful of us? Are we really doing all that? Are students simple lumps of clay to be molded to the form deemed most appropriate by the teacher? Are they glowing pieces of iron that teachers hammer into useful tools? To tell you the truth, I think that we would be presuming too much if we even hinted that teachers are the ones who make changes like those happen. Students are the ones who are the protagonists in the learning process, not the teacher.

The *tabula rasa* metaphor doesn't seem to explain what really happens in teaching and learning. We need to find another metaphor that more closely matches what education is really about. I think I have found one. Here it goes. Let's change the teacher's hammer for a whistle and the lump of clay for an athlete. Yes, that's better. Not new you say? Well of course there are other metaphors, symphony conductor and musicians for example, but since we started this conversation with a sports theme, let's stick with the sports theme. Now in terms of a sports team being led by the coach, what is the role of the athlete? It is to learn and apply what is learned. The coach provides immediate feedback by giving the athletes either individual information concerning performance or general information for the team. Once this is given, the coach says, "Try it again." During each iteration of the skill (or time at bat), the coach gives immediate feedback, but it is the athletes who are willingly sweating, struggling, and expending all that energy. Each time the skill is performed, the athletes improve—they turn themselves into better athletes. Through practice and listening to good coaching (teaching), students increase their stamina, strength, and skill. Most successful coaches do not have to coerce their team members to perform because when athletes see improvement, that is motivation enough to push them to keep on sweating, struggling, and expending all that energy. At times, the coach needs to point out the progress or lack of progress (assessment). If the latter, this is immediately followed by, "Do it over again." Believe it or not, we are now back to where we started. Who is it that is doing the "forming" in formative assessments? It is obvious that it is the athletes. So why do we find it so difficult to use this model in our classrooms?

"We do use this model!" you say.

Respectfully, I ask the following questions. "Students willingly sweat, struggle, and expend all sorts of energy in your classes? You give pretests and posttests so students can judge their performance and measure the improvement? You provide rubrics of expected performance before students are expected to perform? You provide constant immediate feedback regarding students' academic progress? If students don't do well, you let them do it again?"

You may answer that you do some of these things regularly, but if we use the coach and athlete metaphor as a comparison, I believe that all of you would agree that the education that occurs in most classrooms is not nearly as "active" as what happens out on the athletic fields. One of the glaring missing elements in the typical classroom learning cycle is the "formative assessment" process that happens naturally on the athletic field. True formative assessment engages students and puts them in charge of their own learning, much as a bowler is in charge of how he or she bowls.

> *The only way that an assessment can be formative is if the student can learn from the assessment.*

Although information gained from tests and quizzes helps teachers know what, when, and how well to teach, formative assessment should not be solely for the teacher. It should primarily be for the student. The student is the one "forming" himself or herself. The opposite of formative is summative, or "game over" assessment. The critical role of the teacher in formative assessment is to provide the student with feedback *and* the opportunity to improve by repeating the task.[31]

In order for an assessment to be "formative," students must be able to do the three things shown in Figure 8.1.

---

[31]Grant Wiggins, one of the foremost authorities on assessment, wrote an excellent article for Edutopia explaining the need for more formative assessment. Read what he says about "feedback" at www.edutopia.org/authentic-assessment-grant-wiggins

Figure 8.1 Formative Assessment Cycle

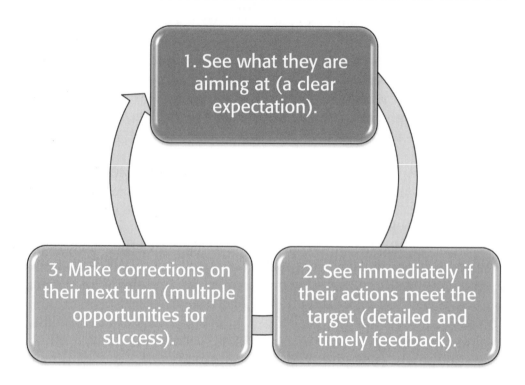

How to Help Students Adjust Based on Feedback

How can students know how to react and adjust to feedback if they receive precious little of it? Our job as educators is to give them as much immediate feedback as we can. This is more than saying, "Good job!" or giving a pat on the back. General verbal feedback has its place, and is essential to a good classroom climate, but the feedback that helps students learn from mistakes is the specific, targeted feedback that illuminates the problem and gives suggestions on how to fix it. For example, a coach might say, "Joe, you're not making the shots because you don't give the ball enough arc. Try it this way and see if it helps." A math teacher might say, "Jessie, you are having trouble with fractions because you might be confusing the numerator with the denominator. Think of it this way: A denominator is like the word denominations. It means types of money. If I give you two of these (you pull out two one-dollar bills and a five-dollar bill), how many one-dollar bills do I have? If this were a fraction, you would write two over five. So the denominator is a type of number that indicates how many pieces a whole is divided into, like five one-dollar bills go into a five-dollar bill. The numerator sits on top and tells how many of the denominators there are. A dollar is how many fifths of a five-dollar bill? So, 2/3 is how many thirds?"

The other feedback that students desperately need comes from formative assessments aligned to the learning standards. Grant Wiggins and Jay McTighe (1998) wrote *Understanding by Design* and explained how teachers need to start with the formative assessment and build learning activities that directly prepare students to be successful. Remember that in order for assessment to be "formative," students have to receive the timely feedback that is specific enough to identify the problem and how to fix it, and then they need to have an opportunity to do it again. A quiz is not formative unless students get the results back promptly and have a chance to take the quiz (the same one or a version of it) again, and if the quiz is aligned then teachers can track student progress by objective.[32]

What kinds of formative assessment can a teacher create to provide immediate feedback to students?

Perhaps the most recognizable formative assessment is having students do a rough draft, which we have already mentioned. In the rough draft process, students submit their first draft for review, then get feedback on their writing, and then make corrections and submit their work again. Though this is time consuming, especially on the first drafts, if the teacher provides effective feedback, later drafts will be much improved and eventually will end up saving time because the students learned (i.e., they know how to do it) and do not need to be reminded in future assignments.

We have already discussed the topic of using questions to prompt students to think analytically, critically, and creatively. As a reminder, asking a verbal question in class and hoping some student will answer it is not the best way to ask questions. For starters, it is not a formative assessment, because it does not provide individual feedback to each student, nor do students have an opportunity to repeat their performance. The other problem with the typical "class discussion model" is that only one student is engaged at a

---

[32] If each question on the quiz correlates to a specific learning objective (one that is also used for the state test), then the data gathered from the quiz will show how your students performed on each objective, and over time will show progress towards mastering the more aligned quizzes you give them. This is what is meant by alignment and it is a powerful concept aided greatly by advances in the technological ability to gather and disaggregate the results by objective. For more information on this topic, see Douglass Reeves's book on assessment. It is an anthology of the best and brightest thought leaders on how to use assessment to improve teaching and learning: Reeves, D. (2007), *Ahead of the curve: The power of assessment to transform teaching and learning.* Bloomington, Indiana: Solution Tree Press.

time. Nevertheless, there are ways to make verbal questioning an excellent formative-assessment method and engage all students. This simple method is to ask all the students to answer the same question at the same time, and then provide individual feedback. (Remember Total Physical Response discussed in chapter 2?)

For example, you could have students give a thumbs-up or thumbs-down gesture in response to a statement you make. They can all touch the correct word on a displayed visual. They can put a finger on the evidence that supports their answer in the book. They can stand up if they think the answer you've given is correct or sit on the floor if they have an answer different from the one you gave. They can stand in one corner if the answer is A or in another corner if it's B. They can lift their right hands for true or left for false. There are many other creative ways to have students all show they understand. TPR is quick, easy, and provides good feedback to the students and teacher. A side product of these techniques is that students also get feedback from looking at what other students are doing, and if they are out of sync with the rest of the class, they usually correct their choices without a teacher having to intervene. Then the correct answer from the teacher simply reinforces what they already learned just moments before. Teachers can tell right away how many students understand and how many don't when they ask students to demonstrate what they know in this way. Then the teacher can immediately adjust instruction to make sure every student understands before going on to the next learning objective.

A similar method makes use of individual electronic keypads, computer programs, "clickers," student polling devices, or even small personal whiteboards, similar to the slates each student had in classrooms long ago. Students write their answers and hold them up so the teacher and all the other students can see.

To help students become flexible and resilient in receiving feedback, they must receive constant sources of feedback. In order for your assessments to be truly formative, you have to set clear standards and expectations of performance, provide detailed and timely feedback, and then give students multiple opportunities to learn from their mistakes to achieve mastery. As teachers, we must provide frequent formative assessments to students so they can see well enough to quit bowling gutter balls and start throwing strikes. Following are some strategies and associated techniques that will help you do this.

S T R A T E G Y

Rough Drafts

Learning takes time and energy on the part of the learner and the teacher. One of the most time intensive yet rewarding strategies available is commonly known as the rough draft. The English language arts folks are well acquainted with this strategy; however, as mentioned earlier, rough drafts can be used in any content area. The concept is basically thus: a student submits a paper fleshed out with ideas and written in readable narrative form. The teacher reads through the paper, bleeds all over it (corrects it with a red pen), makes suggestions for improvement, and returns it to the student. With this new information about the paper, the student can now rewrite the paper, fixing the mistakes. The paper is then resubmitted and corrected cyclically until it is error-free. This may take several iterations, or if the student is a quick study, only one iteration.

TECHNIQUE: Movie critic. Movie critics have to come up with a snazzy line that says what they feel about a movie. When peer reviewing another's work, students come up with their own one-liners about their general impression of the work, taglines for the more in-depth analysis to follow. This forces students to acknowledge the primary strengths and weaknesses in creative, higher-order thinking ways.

"Bring your pillow for this essay full of trite, uninspired ideas!"

"You might need your seatbelt for this rollercoaster of a narrative!"

"The cast of *Law and Order* could not improve on this argument!"

TECHNIQUE: Critique assembly line. One of the things that the assembly line did for the production of automobiles was to create automobiles in a hurry. Each assembly line worker became an expert at the one task he or she was assigned. Assign peer review topics to different teams of students. Each team only reviews for their topic, then passes the papers on to the next team. One benefit of this method is that the reviews will probably be more objective because of so many raters. Before the peer review begins, you may want to perform some inter-rater reliability to make sure all the members of the team evaluate the same topics the same way.

For example, you assign one team of students to check for grammar mistakes, another team to look for supporting evidence, and a third team to evaluate the support of the thesis statements and the conclusion.

TECHNIQUE: Partner review. Have students use the peer review checklist to review a partner's paper. Once completed, the partner will review the other partner's paper. Then the papers are submitted with the reviews, which are also part of the grade.

S T R A T E G Y

Test Retake Policy

The concept behind this strategy is that students must fix the errors they committed on a test, assessment, or evaluation; include explanations (not excuses) of why they got certain parts wrong; and finally, show they have learned by retaking the test, assessment, or evaluation with similar questions to the ones they missed the first time. Formative assessments based on learning objectives are powerful tools for tracking student progress, class progress, and teacher effectiveness on specific learning objectives. What I mean by this is that every question of a quiz is identified with a particular learning objective that was taught in the class. As the instruction proceeds and these aligned assessments are taken, teachers can track student progress (mastery) by objective, which is much more powerful than simply giving students an A, B, or C or percentage grades on the assessment as a whole. While a plethora of data analysis tools exist for disaggregating student performance by objective, it takes the persistence of a dedicated teacher to utilize them consistently. If done correctly, a teacher can know—with more certainty than any district benchmark could provide—how well each of his or her students would perform on the state standardized test.

TECHNIQUE: Same exact test. A convenient method to make student assessment a learning process is to allow students to take the same exact test again to improve the score. However, it is not fair to students who did well on the test and will not be taking the test again if a retaker gets the same points. Therefore, the teacher should set a sliding scale subtracting for the extra study days, or a diminishing percentage depending on the number of times the test can be taken. For example, the first time a test is given, it is worth 100 points. The second time it is worth 80 points. The third time it is worth 70 points. The fourth time it is worth 60 points. You can adjust the scale to suit your purposes. Remember this is for formative assessment and not for summative assessment. We want students to be able to perform well on the formative assessment in preparation for the summative assessment.

TECHNIQUE: Objective-related test. Especially nowadays, teachers have at their disposal item banks of questions that are aligned to certain learning objectives. The only difference from the previous technique is that the test would be a different test, but testing over the same exact objectives. This still allows the results to be disaggregated and compared to the other tests as long as they are all aligned to the same standards. To be fair to students who did not make mistakes, the grading of the corrections should not give students the opportunity for a perfect score, but should allow students to improve their grades to a certain extent.

Chapter

9

Openness to Possible Failure

*Openness to failure: Willingness to
trust and take academic risks*

Why Do Students Need to Be Open to Possible Failure?

I was recently the assistant superintendent of a small school district located just thirty miles south of San Antonio, Texas, with a total school population of 1,100 students. Even though people consider it a rural district, its existence is anything but bucolic. Natalia is a bedroom community for San Antonio, and as such, has to deal with many big-city issues. The population is 75 percent Hispanic, but only about 15 percent of those Hispanic students actually speak Spanish, and a very small percentage of those learned English as a second language. The district's biggest concerns were the achievement gaps that existed between white and Hispanic students and the overall mentality of underachievement. Although I wore many hats in my position, the one that felt most comfortable was the one relating to curriculum and instruction—in particular, helping teachers maximize their instructional power and overcome barriers to student learning.

If you haven't noticed by now, I am a pragmatist, and I believe in simple, systemic solutions. I firmly believe that the true art/skill/magic/science of teaching is to perfectly match your style with the individual student's needs. Conceptually, many teachers know this is the right way to teach. However, it flies in the face of what most teaching professionals practice. Today, more often than not, it is the students who must adapt or fail.

Teaching in the truest sense of the word comes down to what you believe about students and what you believe is the best way to teach them. This is what I believe:

> *Students and teachers working together can achieve substantial learning gains. Teachers working by themselves will achieve nothing.*

As an example of this, I would like to share a short story. A shaggy but beautiful stray dog came to our house one day. Our hearts went out to it, and we decided to help it. We put out some food, which it ate, but it refused to let us approach. Every time we tried, it would shy away and stay out of reach. As much as we wanted to be of more help to the dog, it would not let us. The bottom line is that for one reason or another, it did not trust us. Who knows what its history was? It trusted us enough to eat our food, but that was as far as it went. I am sure that, given a few weeks, we could have built a relationship of trust with that dog—but unfortunately, it moved on and we haven't seen it since.

Students who come to our classrooms are much like that dog (no fleas of course): Unless the students trust us, they are unapproachable. Imagine being asked to ride a two-seater bicycle across a tightrope with somebody you do not trust steering the bicycle. We earn our students' trust by showing them respect in the form of meaningful, challenging, and rewarding learning activities that are worthy of their time and best efforts. This kind of trust has to be developed early in the student's tightrope riding (education) career, otherwise no students in their right mind would attempt it.

Students in their early years of school are naturally trusting, and—please don't take this the wrong way—we often abuse that trust in the name of socialization and classroom management. In order to control large numbers of students at the same time, we teach them to obey rather than to explore. Because of this, as students get older, they often trust less and start behaving much like our shaggy and suspicious visitor. Most will take what we offer but will not allow a lasting learning partnership to develop.

Trust works the other way, too. As teachers, we have learned to distrust our students. All it takes is one disruptive young person to ruin it for the rest of the students who follow. We don't want to get burned again, so we tighten the rules and narrow the focus. We develop an attitude that we can't trust our students to learn independently. Especially in the early grades, we feel it is our responsibility to control every aspect of the learning activities so things don't get out of hand, or so they don't make a mess, or so things do not get too loud.

We could call this way of thinking the color-between-the-lines syndrome: We like everything neat and orderly. So by the time students get to high school, some know how to color between the lines and are successful in school, while others do poorly or drop out because they are not even interested in coloring and will purposely color outside the lines to make their point. Many times, like our beautiful stray dog, students have taken a risk and have been burned, which teaches them to never take a risk again. This is especially evident in math. I had a math teacher who scared me to death. He demanded that we learn the properties and theorems of algebra and be able to recite them word for word when he called our student numbers (not even our names). I was always petrified that he would call on me. To this day, I cringe when I hear the algebraic postulates. Luckily, I had teachers after that who related better to students and math, so much so that I got a math minor in college. Anyway, I know that my algebra teacher meant well—knowing the rules of algebra is essential to being successful in algebra—but the method he used was unsuccessful for me and, I would assume, for many of his students. All too often, students never recover from math or science shock and, as a result, go out of their way to avoid anything related to math or science.

Teachers inhibit risk-taking in other ways without even recognizing that that is what they are doing. For example, by always insisting that students shut up and listen to you, you send the clarion message, "What I have to say is more important than anything you might say." There is no way students can compete with that, and if they try, many times we view their questions as challenges, as being insubordinate and disrespectful. The idea that teachers have all the answers is ludicrous. Equally ludicrous is the prevalent idea that students have none of the answers. I once had a student teacher who taught the introduction to psychology courses at a high school. I gave her an assignment to prepare a pretest and a posttest to one of her psychology lessons. She protested the pretest because, in her words, "My students don't know anything about psychology; it is therefore pointless to test them prior to instruction!" I couldn't believe the arrogance emanating from this teacher.

There is a solution to this: student-centered learning or, better stated, student-directed learning. I say student-directed learning because it is too easy to mistake the idea of focusing all of the teacher's attention on students as student-centeredness. If you as the teacher are making all of the decisions about what to study and how to study it, then it is really teacher-centered learning. As discussed earlier with formative assessments, the student is the one doing the heavy lifting of learning. In order to motivate students and help them be willing to do the sweating, struggling, and energy-expending required of learning, we must allow a certain amount of student independence and choice. Teaching is just as much about taking risks as learning is. A teacher has to take a chance on students and trust them enough to be independent learners. That can't happen if the teacher is uncomfortable about tailoring the curriculum to multiple levels of student performance.[33]

As I stated earlier, teaching styles flow from what an educator believes is the "best way to teach students." That belief is not demonstrated in mission statements and platitudes, but is clearly visible in the way teachers set up and run their classrooms and in how they treat their students. Once a teacher truly understands the mechanics of the learning cycle, discipline and classroom management take a secondary role, and the teacher can focus on what he or she can do to help all of his or her students learn best, whatever it takes. Basic to student-directed learning is that we have to trust students enough to give them formative learning opportunities we sometimes call assessments. We have to trust students to master content sufficiently in order to collaborate with their peers on project-based learning, investigations, explorations, and inquiry. We have to trust that students, given the right learning environment, will learn. We have to show trust in our students as the protagonists of the learning process by providing them opportunities to show what they have learned rather than always depending on paper and pencil assessment. Above all, we need to develop that trust in the early grades. Otherwise, we will end up trying unsuccessfully to teach a bunch of skittish stray dogs for students.

How to Help Students Be Open to Possible Failure

As discussed earlier, trust is the basic element of any relationship, but it is even more so for teaching and learning. When students trust their teachers, they can be more frank with their vulnerabilities. And such lucky teachers, because of that trust, can push these students to higher standards than would ordinarily be possible. One of the college- and career-readiness skills that university professors who participated in the University of Oregon study on

---

[33]Although differentiation is not necessarily a strategy to help teachers to prepare students to be college- and career-ready, it is a way to promote individual student success by catering instruction to their needs. Carol Anne Tomlinson, the queen of differentiation, has written several informative books that should be part of your professional library. Here is the one you really should have: Tomlinson, C. A. (2001). *How to differentiate instruction in mixed ability classrooms* (2nd Ed.). Alexandria, VA: Association for Supervision and Curriculum Development.

college-readiness wish their students had is the ability to face the fact that they will not succeed at everything. Sometimes students will fail (English, 2000).[34] Students will face multitudes of obstacles they will have to overcome in order to be successful; they cannot afford to wimp out at the first sign of trouble. Unfortunately, too many students do not recover from failure, as demonstrated in the 2003 statistics from the ACT report called *Reading Between the Lines: What the ACT Reveals About College Readiness in Reading*. More than 3,000 students drop out of high school every day, primarily because they do not possess the literacy skills to keep up with the curriculum. Even students who make it to college are not able to face failures. Eleven percent of students in college are enrolled in remedial reading coursework, and 75 percent of them will not obtain their degree in eight years (ACT, 2006).

Learning involves opening up and exposing our vulnerability, trusting, taking risks, and becoming resilient about the outcomes. Taking risks involves many complex psychological and behavioral functions. One of the things that I learned as a foreign-language teacher is that each person has what is called an affective filter ("affective" meaning dealing with emotions). When we feel intimidated or afraid of how others will respond, or have a fear of being spotlighted, our affective filter clamps down, thinking stops, and we are left with the primal fight or flight choices. According to neuroscientists, this is a physiological response to an infusion of cortisol, a neuropeptide that inhibits logic function by blocking transmission of neural messages in the hippocampus (this is the organ that is associated strongly with learning and memory). What this means is that when we experience strong negative emotion, cortisol is released and the thinking part of the brain is inhibited, leaving us with the primal part of the brain that worries only about survival. Constant stress, or chronic stress, can lead to destruction of neurons in the hippocampus that Bill Cosby would call "brain damage" (see Figure 9.1).

As we've discussed earlier, students are fairly adept at avoiding and minimizing their exposure to situations in which they are placed in the public spotlight. For this reason, they sit in the back of the room, they do not raise their hands, and they basically keep a low profile in your classroom. In previous chapters, we've also discussed the traditional teacher-questioning routine: ask a general question and let whichever students raise their hands first answer it. In general, we know who those students are. There is an easy fix for lowering the affective filter so students do not need to hide in your classroom.

---

[34]One of the problems with our system is the bell curve because it assumes that we are satisfied with a majority of our students being mediocre and 15% of our students failing entirely. Fenwick English describes how we should have a skewed bell curve that targets a higher percentage of highly proficient students rather than just 15% at the top.

Figure 9.1 Effects of Cortisol on the Hypocampus (Jasmin Johnson, 2012)

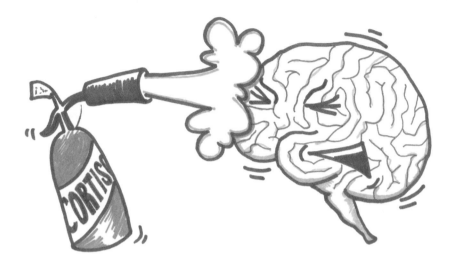

The most effective way to reduce the affective filter is to reduce the size of the audience. For students, it is much easier to make mistakes in front of one or two students than to be exposed to the ridicule of the whole class witnessing inadequacies and failures. As teachers, we must be sensitive to the climate of the class and the levels of stress that it maintains.

This does not mean that all stress is bad. There is another type of stress called *Eustress* that is good stress and makes our bodies respond in a positive manner. *Eustress* is experienced by students when they are given challenging circumstances but they feel prepared to face them with confidence. In this case, another neuropeptide is released called endorphins. Athletes feel the effects of endorphins during workouts. This is sometimes known as the "runner's high," not surprisingly because this peptide mimics the effects of opiates to reduce pain and increase a sense of euphoria.[35] We need to make sure our learning environment and learning activities minimize "stress," or challenges for which students are unprepared, and instead prepare students to be successful in rigorous learning challenges so that eustress can reduce anxiety and make them stronger. The key to developing college- and career-ready students is to cultivate in the students a state of relaxed alertness.

---

[35] Robert Sylwester is an Emeritus Professor of Education at the University of Oregon. He is coauthor of the Information Age Education bimonthly Newsletter available at http://i-a-e.org. The information about peptides and their effect on the brain came from his early book on the brain. If you want to understand more of how the student (and our) brain works, you will want to read this book: Sylwester, R. (1995) *A celebration of neurons: An educator's guide to the human brain*. Alexandria, VA: Association for Supervision and Curriculum Instruction.

S T R A T E G Y

Tell Students That It Will Be Hard, But They Can Do It

Yes, it is as simple as that. I read a study that had two groups of students of similar mixes of abilities, backgrounds, and socioeconomic status. One group was told that they were going to be given very hard tasks and that they would be able to do them. The other group was told nothing. Both groups were given the same instruction and the same tasks. Guess which group did best? Simply priming the pump for success builds success.

S T R A T E G Y

Pretesting

Research has been done to determine if pretesting does any good or, perhaps a better way to put it, if failing to answer questions correctly on a pretest poses an inhibitor of future learning. The findings are conclusive. Pretesting not only provides a preview of future learning and sets up a scaffold into which the future knowledge can be placed, but it also helps students learn better. The tests that were performed had three groups of college students. One group was given extra time to study a specially-prepared text with bolded key words. Another group was given a pretest, and the final group was the control group. When the results were analyzed, the pretest group outscored the group that was given extra study time with the bolded key words, even after a week of separation.[36] Pretesting has other benefits too. It

---

[36] Three researchers from the University of California, Irvine and Los Angeles, performed a series of five tests to determine if failing a pretest made it harder to learn. What they discovered was powerful. Not only was the opposite true, but each of the tests supported that pretesting was more effective than other proven methods to enhance knowledge retention such as providing

makes sure that the instructor covers what the instructor says he is going to cover. Too often teachers make up the test after instruction has occurred, which leaves room for gaps in content due to instructors bird-walking (getting off topic, or spending inordinate amounts of time on pet topics). A pretest lets the students know what is important to remember, and even though they fail the pretest, the exposure will aid long-term memory of the content as long as the teacher makes sure that it is covered. (If they pass the pretest, then the teacher should be smart enough to skip that section and go on to the next one.)

TECHNIQUE: Same test. As Grant Wiggins proposes, teachers who take the time to prepare the assessments beforehand automatically know what the targeted learning for the day will be. When the teacher gives students the pretest, then students will know what they are supposed to learn. If the same test that is given as a pretest is given as a posttest, then the results can be directly compared, and students and the teacher will know exactly what progress was made.

TECHNIQUE: Form A & B. The form A can be given as a pretest, and the form B given as a posttest, only if the questions on test A are correlated directly with the same learning objectives used for the test form B.

---

extra study time, italicizing key words, bolding key words, and the teacher emphasizing the words. Even a week later, the pretested students performed better. Attempting to answer a question on a pretest and failing at it helps students learn when the information is actually taught to them later. See: Richland, L., Kornell, N., & Kao, L. (2009). The pretesting effect: do unsuccessful retrieval attempts enhance learning?. *Journal Of Experimental Psychology. Applied,* 15(3), 243-257. Retrieved from MEDLINE with Full Text database.

SECTION III
CONCLUSION

Building Resiliency Is Like Broccoli

Active learning is like broccoli. Learning is hard work. It takes time and energy to learn. It takes brainpower, concentration, and diligence. It takes monotonous repetition, over and over again. Active learning is like broccoli.

Active learning is like broccoli. Even when students know that it is for their own good, their futures, and their lives, learning doesn't get any easier. It is an investment in time and energy. It is a sacrifice of what is wanted now, for a better future later. Active learning is like broccoli.

Actually, this was the conclusion of two researchers, Veronica Smith and LeeAnn Cardaciotto (2011). They conclude, "It appears that active learning may indeed be like broccoli: Although it is good for students intellectually, their overall impression of it may not be completely positive" (p. 58). What these two researchers did to determine this amazing truth was to look at students in large lectures classes in psychology. They worked with the lecturer and devised extended learning activities following the lecture. One half of the students participated in "Active Learning" that "required the students to reflect, evaluate, analyze, synthesize, and communicate on or about the lesson" (p. 54). The other half did "Content Review" activities that you would find at the end of a textbook chapter. What they discovered was that the active learning group performed much better in the class but were not as enthusiastic as other groups about the class. Broccoli is good for us, full of nutrients, yet young people still shy away from eating it. The truth about learning is that it is hard work and, understandably, active learning may be perceived to be even harder work.

Speaking of hard work, another researcher demonstrates that even geniuses have to work hard when it comes to learning. Dr. Carol Dweck (2010), a professor of psychology at Stanford, explains that there are two mindsets when it comes to learning: a growth mindset and a fixed mindset. Her research has led her to believe that students who have developed a growth mindset are much more capable of being resilient learners than those who harbor a fixed mindset. The students with the fixed mindset may be brilliant, but they assume that their brilliance is limited and are careful to not engage in learning behaviors that may diminish this perception of brilliance. The students with a growth mindset may be just as brilliant but are willing to take learning risks to acquire more knowledge and skills. (As a side note, the fixed mindset kind of thinking is one of the dangers of the "personality profiles" that calculate a student's color or psychological status. There is the implicit message that the profile is set and teachers and students have to deal with it, but in reality, an indication of a preference does not mean that students cannot adapt and learn to behave in different profiles). Dr. Dweck proposes that teachers create a climate of growth mindset through reinforcement of specific growth mindset behaviors such as persistence, application of learning strategies, and level of effort. Specific praise on their behavior is much more powerful than telling students they are smart. Teachers can actually instruct students about the two mindsets and explore with them the behaviors that lead to each (see *www.brainology.us* for more info on this). Goal setting is a growth mindset behavior that, when applied to individual student learning, can help them go for the challenging learning goals rather than the minimum. Dr. Dweck emphasizes challenge rather than success by providing a differentiated set of activities in order to help those brilliant students from coasting. She also suggests that simply providing students with a before and an after picture establishes that through hard work, learning growth is the result.

Section IV

Creating Communicators

Effective Vocabulary Development Is the Basis for Effective Communication

 When I was an administrator in a small school district, I faced the challenge of diminishing the achievement gap in the student scores, especially in math and science. For example, we noticed that in science there was a 40 point-gap between the number of Hispanic students passing the test versus the number of Anglo students passing. This meant that the average of all Hispanic students' scores on the science test was 40 percentage points below the average of all Anglo students' scores. Having been in the classrooms and having witnessed the teachers teaching, I knew for a fact that they were not treating the Hispanic students any differently from the Anglo students. Also, I knew that the Hispanic students were neither more nor less intelligent than the Anglo students. Even more perplexing was the fact that the school district was composed of 70% Hispanics and only 25% Anglo. Of those Hispanic students, surprisingly few of them ever had been or were classified as ESL. Almost all of them spoke English fluently. So why was there an achievement gap?

The academic teams wrestled with this question for a while, but one day, when I was talking with my own children, it dawned on me what the problem was. Having been an educator for a while, I sometimes had to watch how I spoke with my own children because they would give me funny looks when I used "big" or unfamiliar words. My own children spoke English just fine, but they did not understand words like *ubiquitous*, *soporiphic*, *loquacious*, or *facetious*. The solution was looking me in the face. I had to ask myself, "Were the teachers teaching using 'academic' speech that the Anglo students were more familiar with than the Hispanic students?"

To make a long story short, the academic teams decided to increase the level of vocabulary development, primarily using many sheltered language techniques borrowed from ESL teaching and learning concepts. The results were astounding. Because of this and an intense college-readiness focus, in two years, our schools went from unacceptable to recognized and then the next year to exemplary.

We learned a few things in the process of increasing the vocabulary readiness of our students. Notice that I did not say that we diminished the "academic" language of the teachers. The focus was on helping students understand and speak the "academic" language. Sheltered instruction is designed with the idea of helping teachers of regular subjects accommodate for English language learners in their classrooms. A close look at the strategies and the techniques of sheltered instruction will reveal that many of them are suitable for all classes. One of the foundations of sheltered instruction is "comprehensible input." What this means is that when the teacher is speaking to the students, the teacher should use multiple contextual clues that provide meaning along with the spoken words. A teacher would use the words verbally, but at the same time point to the objects being described, and also show the words in written format. Gestures, pantomime, movement, actions, sounds, pictures, graphics, and video all are additional methods that teachers have at their disposal to increase the likelihood that their students will understand the message. At about the same time, we came across Marzano's *Building Background Knowledge*, which basically states that before a student can grasp the concepts being taught, the student needs a mental scaffold in which to place them. Experience, first-hand or virtual, is the number one scaffold-building tool. Reading is second best, and the next best tool is intense vocabulary development prior to instruction.

As a Spanish teacher, I learned early on that the mouth is connected to the brain, and if the mouth cannot say the word, then there is little chance that the brain will remember it. Learning new content in math or science is much like learning in a conversational Spanish class. If done right, students will leave the class being fluent in the language and culture of science or they will be able to converse in the language of math. This requires that the teacher realize that students may not understand completely what *reduce, simplify, analyze, compute, illustrate,* or *group* means. In the Mix It Up Correlated Math and Science program from Texas State University, they have discovered that some of the math terminology frequently means something else in science. For example, "accuracy" in math may refer to the number of decimal places of a number, but in science it may refer to the preciseness of the measuring device (i.e., grams vs. milligrams).

The best way I have learned to build vocabulary is beginning with a visual/verbal/aural Bloom-ish scaffolding method—starting easy then getting more complex and difficult. Here are some methods:

♦ **Recognition of the word in context:** As I point to the endoplasmic reticulum picture, I say, "Is this an endoplasmic reticulum?" The students say in unison, "Yes." As I point to a picture of a ribosome, I say, "Is this a vacuole?" Hopefully they respond, "No." As a TPR methodology, I can ask them to stand next to or point to the mitochondria or chloroplasts.

◆ **Reproduction of the words in context:** After going through all of the words, I ask students to say the words, "What is this?" as I point to the nucleus. After I am satisfied they can say the words, I check their understanding, "Which organelle of the cell processes energy for the nucleus?" (mitochondria/chloroplasts) "Which parts of the cell are necessary to create proteins?" (endoplasmic reticulum, nucleus, golgi apparatus, and ribosomes)

◆ **Written words in context:** I then bring out the written word strips and ask students to match them with the pictures. Then and only then will I let students start reading the chapters, or workbooks, because not only are they now familiar with the concepts, but they have muscle memory of the words in their mouths and know how to say them and thus remember them. This method is more enjoyable and more effective for students than writing the words ten times each in sentences . . . an all too typical vocabulary development technique.

Possessing adequate vocabulary is fundamental to any form of communication in any discipline. Teachers must consider development of not only content vocabulary, but also process vocabulary associated with the content. College- and career-ready students not only have a burgeoning academic vocabulary, but they also have strategies to increase their vocabulary through reading and writing strategies.

> *"Writing today is not a frill for the few, but an essential skill for the many."*
>
> (NATIONAL COMMISSION ON WRITING IN AMERICA'S SCHOOLS AND COLLEGES, 2003)

Chapter 10

Ability to Express Oneself in Writing and Orally

Communicate: Convey meaning in such a way that it is understood

Why Do Students Need to Communicate Effectively?

The controversial author Norman Mailer said, "I don't know what I think until I write it down." Another famous author, Joan Didion, perhaps said it better in this way: "I write entirely to find out what I'm thinking, what I'm looking at, what I see and what it means. What I want and what I fear." Donald Murray, a pioneer of the writing process, stated, ". . . all writers 'are compelled to write to see what their words tell them'" (as quoted in Stewart, 2011, p. 50).

Learning from what you write. There is an amazing power to learn when you read what you have written. When we write to learn, we analyze, we revise, we organize, we rewrite, we evaluate, and so on until what is written is what we want to communicate. These are all higher-order thinking skills that we aspire to achieve in the classroom setting. The way it works for me is that I start with an idea and write it down. Then, if I get stuck, I play with it (sometimes like a cat with a dead mouse); I add to it, take away from it, and shift it until it makes sense to me. Sometimes I have to let it sit for a while. One of my students said she lets it "marinate." Thinking is hard work. Writing to learn is hard thinking.

The first level of writing to learn has already been discussed in the critical reading section of this book. Critical reading happens when students read the stellar works of authors and try to understand not only what was written, but also the implications from what messages are being portrayed by the word choices, style, tone, and organization of the text. What better way to clarify understanding than to use writing to enhance learning! Schmoker (2006) affirms that a great way to write to learn is reading with "pen in hand," ready to jot down notes in the margins (or on a note pad if you have an aversion to writing in books), in order to capture the things we want to remember: corollary thoughts, disagreements, questions, things to look up for more research, evidence, words we do not understand, references, or more. As mentioned earlier, Cornell Notes provide a way to use writing to enhance learning and thinking. Overall, however, it is not specifically the writing that helps the learning; it is the thinking. Though writing is an active-learning endeavor, not passive as in listening, the act of writing involves more of the entire body in the process and thus increases the likelihood of learning. What makes the writing to learn powerful is the process of reading, thinking, writing, rereading, and rewriting that occurs over time.

Writing to learn is more than just putting words on the page for someone else to read. The focus has to be on what the writer gets out of the process of writing, not just the reader. The process of writing to learn clarifies perspectives and crystalizes jewels of personal beliefs. The final product of the writing to learn process is a summation of the thinking and learning that occurred.

Students begin to write to learn by laboriously reading what others have written and then mimicking their style and methods in their own writing. As students get more sophisticated in their writing and learning, they will be able to reflect on their learning: what was learned and what was not learned, how it was learned, and perhaps why. Just as the Common Core State Standards rely on critical reading skills as foundations for all learning, critical writing holds a prominent position. For example, four of the ten CCSS College and Career Readiness Anchor Standards for writing that specifically require critical writing are listed in Figure 10.1.

On the continuum of critical writing where you have writing for fun vs. writing to learn, perhaps the ultimate writing to learn would be the point at which students arrive at reflexiveness. No, this has nothing to do with that little trianglar rubber hammer tap and the knee-jerk reaction. Reflexiveness is when the students challenge their own writing and learning by asking hard questions about what they think and what they believe and how that affects their writing. Questions like: Why do I believe this? What evidence do I have that supports my belief? Does this demonstrate a personal bias?

Figure 10.1 CCSS Critical Writing

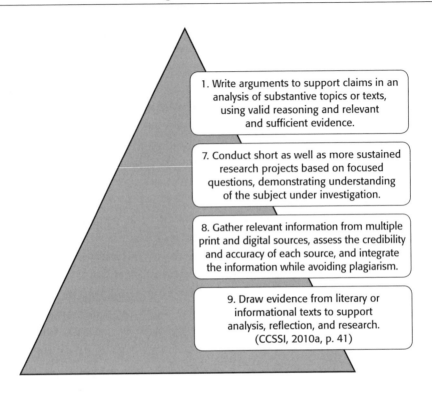

1. Write arguments to support claims in an analysis of substantive topics or texts, using valid reasoning and relevant and sufficient evidence.

7. Conduct short as well as more sustained research projects based on focused questions, demonstrating understanding of the subject under investigation.

8. Gather relevant information from multiple print and digital sources, assess the credibility and accuracy of each source, and integrate the information while avoiding plagiarism.

9. Draw evidence from literary or informational texts to support analysis, reflection, and research. (CCSSI, 2010a, p. 41)

What fallacies in thinking am I succumbing to? According to Kingdon (2005), reflexivity is acknowledging the researcher's own standpoint or theoretical perspective. Yes, that is right, reflexivity is usually only learned about in the university setting of research writing, but if you think about it, research writing is the pinnacle of writing to learn.

When I first heard of reflexivity in my doctoral studies, I thought that the professor had said it wrong. "Certainly he meant reflectivity!" I thought. But as I questioned him, he explained that the research reflex action is different from a reflect action. Reflectivity only requires the writer to review what has happened, and perhaps analyze it to arrive at some understanding, point of view, or course of action. Reflexivity requires the writer to reflect and then determine what effect he himself has on the thinking and writing that is taking place. This includes evaluating his own personal character and beliefs and, in essence, includes assessing the effects of "who the writer is" on "what is being written." The idea of reflexivity also takes into account that identifying this effect on writing might be a moving target. We all have our own personal biases and preferences, and these, along with our values and perspectives, shape how we view and interpret the world. Reflexivity does not involve eradication of those things; it is simply an acknowledgement of them that may bring the writer to new insights and greater personal understanding, and ultimately make the writing more clear and forceful.

For example, students reading *To Kill a Mockingbird* are exposed to prejudice in a number of different forms. Reflective writing would be to put themselves in the shoes of Scout or Atticus or Boo and discover what their own responses would be. Reflexive writing would take that one step further. It would require students to identify their sympathies, biases, and their own prejudices and identify how these affect their personal analysis of the book.

Using writing as a way to learn affixes writing firmly back into the trinity of the three Rs. A 2006 panel on writing stated that writing was the most neglected curriculum.[37] How could that be? From kindergarten on, students are constantly writing. The lifeblood of schools depends on paper and pencil activities. But are those activities purposeful efforts to develop narrative, expository, and argument skills? Probably not. Never fear, the CCSS have come to the rescue. From kindergarten on, purposeful writing is part of the plan.

How to Help Students Express Themselves in Writing and Orally

As students learn the mechanics of writing, cursively or not, the default mode of writing is always *narrative*. Only much later in their writing careers are students exposed to the other two forms of writing: *explanatory* and *argument*. Is it wrong to have elementary students write explanatory papers or arguments along with their narrative writing? The Common Core State Standards hold that students need to be doing all three even as students are learning the mechanics of writing letters and words. The CCSS ELA College and Career Readiness Anchor Standards for Writing are shown in Figure 10.2.

As we've discussed, clarity of writing depends on clarity of thinking. The standard writing cycle is described as planning for writing, writing, and revising writing. It sounds so simple, yet why do students all over the United States have difficulty writing?

---

[37] The National Commission on Writing in America's Schools and Colleges authored a report in 2006 titled, *Writing and school reform: The neglected "r"* and earlier wrote a report in 2003 titled, *The neglected "r": The need for a writing revolution.* Both of these reports are foundational for every teacher and can be obtained from the College Board website at www.host-collegeboard.com/advocacy/writing/publications.html. Within the reports, you will find excellent resources and ideas for increasing writing in your classrooms.

Figure 10.2 CCSS Writing Anchor Standards
(Including sub-genres. See CCSSI, 2010c, p. 6)

Text Types and Purposes
1. Write arguments to support claims in an analysis of substantive topics or texts, using valid reasoning and relevant and sufficient evidence.
2. Write informative/explanatory texts to examine and convey complex ideas and information clearly and accurately through the effective selection, organization, and analysis of content.
3. Write narratives to develop real or imagined experiences or events using effective technique, well-chosen details, and well-structured event sequences.
Production and Distribution of Writing
4. Produce clear and coherent writing in which the development, organization, and style are appropriate to task, purpose, and audience.
5. Develop and strengthen writing as needed by planning, revising, editing, rewriting, or trying a new approach.
6. Use technology, including the Internet, to produce and publish writing and to interact and collaborate with others.
Research to Build and Present Knowledge
7. Conduct short as well as more sustained research projects based on focused questions, demonstrating understanding of the subject under investigation.
8. Gather relevant information from multiple print and digital sources, assess the credibility and accuracy of each source, and integrate the information while avoiding plagiarism.
9. Draw evidence from literary or informational texts to support analysis, reflection, and research.
Range of Writing
10. Write routinely over extended time frames (time for research, reflection, and revision) and shorter time frames (a single sitting or a day or two) for a range of tasks, purposes, and audiences.

Lawrence Musgrove, an associate professor of English and foreign languages at Saint Xavier University in Chicago, had this to say about why students have trouble writing:

> When I find significant errors in student writing, I chalk it up to one of three reasons: they don't care, they don't know, or they didn't see it. And I believe that the first and last are the most frequent causes of error. In other words, when push comes to shove, I've found that *most students really do know how to write*—that is, if we can help them learn to value and care about what they are writing and then help them manage the time they need to compose effectively.

He added that a large part of the problem with the low writing standards is that most of his colleagues would rather complain about poor writing than refuse to accept it. He compared it to driving a car. The reasons to be a good driver are obvious: everyone knows the rules, and consequences are enforced. As a solution to the problem, he maintains that if every college teacher challenged the writing proficiency of every student, it would in essence force the rules of the road out into the open, and students would be held accountable for good writing.[38]

I would take Dr. Musgrove's interesting perspective of the problem one step further. If students really do not know how to write, the problem is not writing. The problem is that they do not know how to think, and they do not know how to use writing to help their thinking. We have plenty of tools and resources to help students learn how to write and how to think. What we are lacking many times is the will and the collective determination to help students care about good writing in every class they take. One of the best ways to help students care about good writing is to give them something to write about that interests them. This doesn't mean that students should not write about things that do not interest them. What it means is that we should provide students with strategies on how to write about things for which they do not have interest by finding an aspect of the topic that can make it interesting for them. Fortunately, we have already discussed how students can employ creativity, critical thinking, and analytical thinking to reading, and interestingly enough, these skills also apply to writing.

College-ready writers are able to write clear narratives, descriptive expository statements, and convincing arguments. But this ability did not ap-

---

[38]Dr. Musgrove goes into more detail on the consequences, such as handing out writing tickets that are attached to the grade in the class and the academic transcript. Too many tickets and the student must attend a remedial writing class or put graduation in jeopardy. See his post on Inside Higher Ed, "The Real Reasons Students Can't Write," April 28th, 2006. Also read some of the comments to get a full dose of the issue. www.insidehighered.com/views/2006/04/28/musgrove

pear all of a sudden. It actually began in kindergarten when the teacher wrote the words down for the student until he could write them himself. The most important part of writing is the thinking that is put into the writing cycle. The planning to write, the actual wording choice, and the revising all require analytical thinking, critical thinking, and most importantly, creative thinking.

As students develop their writing skills—starting with the actual mechanics of forming letters, composing words, and combining those words into sentences—certain prewriting strategies can help them engage the brain as well as their fine motor skills. One of the best methods books for grades one through four is the *Four Square Writing Method* (Gould & Gould, 1999; 2002). The basic premise of the Four Square Writing Method is to use a planning template made of a square cut in four parts. In the center of the square is a smaller box that holds the topic, while three of the quadrants contain paragraph detail sentences. The lower-right quadrant contains a "feeling" sentence. Completion of the template helps students plan what kinds of things should be included in a paragraph, and also helps them make sure the details support the central topic. Successful completion of a Four Square Writing Template gives students at least one sentence per quadrant, plus the topic sentence, for a total of five sentences. Frankly, there is no reason that the planning of paragraph writing using this method could not be extended all the way through high school. It is that straightforward and that effective. Any of the three main genres of writing work with this template.

Once the planning is done using Four Square, the outline method, or another method, then the actual writing can be done. Writing more than one paragraph means that not only does each paragraph need a central theme, but there also has to be a unifying theme connecting all of the paragraphs. Tying paragraphs together requires the use of connecting words and phrases. The five-paragraph format is the basic organization technique for most writing genres. College-ready students are fluent in the different genres of writing, recognizing that newspaper writing has its own organization strategy that differs from scholarly writing, just as a narrative differs from an argument. The college-ready student will be able to capitalize on the similarities shared by the genres. For example, the strategy of supporting beliefs and opinions by using evidence drawn from research or personal experience is as powerful in narratives as it is in arguments. Once the thinking and connecting of paragraphs is done, then two things can happen: the revision process or the verbal presentation of a report, of research findings, of an argument, etc. College-ready students are capable of verbally presenting their ideas. Though the general structure of spoken language and written language are the same, where they differ is related to how the brain assimilates the knowledge. In writing, the reader can go back and read what it says in order to get clarification. In oral presentations, that is not possible. Therefore accommodations must be made to help listeners keep the main points in their working memory: fewer numbers of points, repetition of the points, and review of the points.

Speaking of working memory, as a child I loved to play the recording by Danny Kaye of the story of the animal village. This is one of those stories for listeners rather than readers because the working memory processes for reading are different from those for listening. As the story is retold, all the animals are hungry, and a magic tree in the village has multitudes of all kinds of ripe fruit. But the tree will only let the fruit fall if the villagers can say the name of the tree. The problem is that none of the villagers can remember it. So they send the fastest, strongest, cleverest, and, believe it or not, slowest animals one by one up to the top of the mountain to talk to the Chief over the Mountains. Each in turn returns to the bottom of the hill having forgotten the special name of the tree. The slowest animal was a turtle of course, and he had a strategy for remembering the name of the tree. Over the course of the story, the name of the tree is repeated several times as each animal fails. Unbeknownst to the listeners, the repetition keeps the name of the tree in their working memory. The turtle and the listeners are able to remember the name of the tree by the end of the story.[39]

Now back to oral delivery. Another form of delivery is very effective in preparing students to be college-ready communicators. This form is the debate. I have found debate to be a magnificent learning tool that engages students (sometimes too much, which is why you need to control the rules of the debate so it doesn't turn into an argument or a brawl), and it helps them clarify their thinking. I know of one school district that is having great success with debates. Kerri Allen is the Resource Development and Communications Manager for the National Association for Urban Debate Leagues in Chicago, and she shared with me the excellent success that students in Chicago are obtaining academically because of being actively involved in the debating league. These debate teams are composed mainly of minority, economically disadvantaged students, yet because of their participation in debate, they enjoy a 90% high school graduation rate as compared to 70% for their peers, and a senior grade point average of 3.23 as compared to 2.8 (3.0 being the established predictor of college success). ACT and SAT scores are higher, and

---

[39] Danny Kaye was a comedic actor who portrayed some of the most humorous roles in the forties and fifties: *The Inspector General* is one of my favorites. In the vinyl record that I listened to hundreds of times, he masterfully told the Tale of the Name of the Tree, a Bantu folktale. For more information on Danny Kaye, see: www.pbs.org/wnet/americanmasters/episodes/danny-kaye/about-the-actor/504/

the increased vocabulary (we discussed this already), as well as the skills of supporting argument with evidence, tremendously increase the likelihood of success in college.[40]

Technique summary for critical writing: Mimicry of Writing, Schmoker's Read with Pen in Hand, Cornell Notes, Reflective Writing, and Reflexive Writing.

S T R A T E G Y

Debate

A marvelous movie with Denzel Washington called the *Great Debaters* demonstrates the power of debate as an educational tool to prepare students to be college-ready communicators. Aside from showing the drama and conflict of the times, it displays the rigorous training that a debate team had to embrace in order to be prepared intellectually, to argue a point of view, to speak clearly and authoritatively, and to think critically on a moment's notice. Following are techniques that you can use in your classroom to make debate a college-readiness tool.

TECHNIQUE: *Four corners.* An effective debate mixer is the four corners method. The teacher displays a topic on the whiteboard/overhead/ SMART Board and assigns a different position relative to that topic to each

---

[40]Researchers from several East Coast colleges completed a ten-year study (1997 to 2006) of over 9,000 students of the Chicago Public Schools. They determined that even though programs like Gear Up and Trio abound, little evidence exists to show that they increase the likelihood of college readiness. They did find one program in the Chicago Public Schools that does prepare students for college in dramatic ways. This is the after-school debate program. Students participating in the program must prepare arguments over agreed upon topics and present them in a 90 minute forum where judges determine the strength and validity of their arguments as well as the style of presentation. The study compared peer groups not in debate with the debate students, and the results show clearly that comparison bell curves for the debate students are all skewed to the right by at least one standard deviation. This means that debate students did better in math, in reading, ACT scores and general GPA than the control group. Mezuk, B., Bondarenko, I. , Smith, S., & Tucker, E. (2011). Impact of participating in a policy debate program on academic achievement: Evidence from the Chicago Urban Debate League. Educational Research and Reviews 6 (9) pp. 622-635. Retrieved May 6, 2012 from www.academicjournals.org/ERR

corner of the room. Students then choose to stand in the corner that best reflects their personal opinion on the matter. Once the corners have been chosen, the teacher gives the students five minutes to create their discussion platform for supporting their position. The debate or pseudo debate begins with each team presenting its opening argument. Then each team has time for presenting evidence and rebuttals, and then there are closing arguments.

TECHNIQUE: Partner. In training for debates, some students are extremely shy and may work better with just one partner rather than a whole group. The process is the same as the four corners technique, but the debate is between two people, not the whole class.

TECHNIQUE: Devil's advocate. This is a twist on the debate positions preparation. Instead of just supporting their own opinion and platform, students will also try their best to throw kinks into their supporting argument. So in essence, instead of just preparing one argument "pro," they also have to prepare one "contra."

TECHNIQUE: Worst case scenario. This is another take-off on the debate platform preparation. To prepare to support their position, students look into the future at the worst possible thing that could happen as a result of the opposing argument. They prepare their defense from that point on.

TECHNIQUE: Glass half empty or half full. This is a technique to help students view the different perspectives and prepare for arguments from each. Students look at their platform from a positivistic point of view and from a pessimistic point of view.

TECHNIQUE: Magic wand. As discussed earlier, the magic wand can eliminate the constraints of reality. In addition, the teacher can bequeath wands that have certain limitations. For example, a wand may make people under 25 years of age 20% smarter than they were before. Students would then have to adjust their platform argument to accommodate this peculiar restriction. The restrictive wands can work with green eyes, other student characteristics, or students from a particular class or teacher.

Chapter 11

Skilled at Information Gathering

Research: Seeking the truth

Why Do Students Need to Be Good Researchers?

Students file into the classroom and are greeted warmly by the teacher at the door. They sit down, and the teacher closes the door behind them. This activity happens daily across the United States and is cause for serious concern. Once that door closes, the students and teacher are a completely isolated microcosm. This physical separation from the rest of the school, although worrisome, is not the most dangerous form of isolation. This chapter seeks to discuss the effects of information isolation on teacher and student scholarship, educational practice, and learning leadership.

Since the inception of public education, the compartmentalization of teaching has had significant repercussions for students and teachers alike. One of the most fundamental results has been the continual decline of teacher scholarship. Michael Schmoker, in his book *Results Now: How We Can Achieve Unprecedented Results in Teaching and Learning*, decries teacher isolation as the main culprit in slipping student and teacher performance (Schmoker, 2006). The problem is even more serious than that. Because of that isolation, teachers neglect their research about how to become better teachers, symbolically closing essential pedagogical doors. The resulting intellectual isolation prohibits and discourages information literacy. The report from the American Library Association (2006) illustrates the dangers of not having appropriate knowledge of current educational research. "Information prepackaging in schools and through broadcast and print news media, in fact, encourages people to accept the opinions of others without much thought. When opinions are biased, negative, or inadequate for the needs at hand, many people are left helpless to improve the situation confronting them" (p. 7). Without solid research to guide them, educators are prone to choose educational solutions based on what the salesmen say and not what is known to be true about teaching and learning.

Teachers know, for example, that good teaching depends on dynamic educational learning environments. Today's students are not the same as the students of a few years ago. Today's students need different sets of knowledge and skills than their parents did. Yet tradition, routine, and ingrained instructional procedures dictate that these students be taught the same things, the same way, as prior students. This security blanket of sameness lulls the teachers and students into a false sense of satisfaction and complacency. Ultimately, if teachers are not careful, they stop being scholars of their craft and become pure practitioners only, dependent on what others decide are sound pedagogical principles.

Teachers who are solely practitioners are confined to what knowledge and skills are currently within their experience. Such teachers are stifled and stuck with their set of "tried and true" teaching strategies. Therefore, because students and their needs are different, and their "tried and true" techniques are less than effective, these teachers must resort to heavy-handed discipline to keep a semblance of learning in their classrooms.

Fortunately, better ways exist for teachers to inspire learning. Teachers must be practitioners, but if they also open themselves to becoming informationally-literate scholars, then they will gain valuable skills and abilities to better provide similar learning experiences for their students. For example, if a teacher and the school librarian collaborate more on the skills required in information literacy, then students will be better equipped to find kernels of truth in the content area, and the information literacy of the teachers will increase, too.

This is not without challenges in the public school arena. The same problems that K–12 public schools have with information literacy are also shared by colleges. According to Zabel,[41] "Undergraduates typically make little use

---

[41] I picked out a theme from the article written by Zabel (2004), "A Reaction to Information Literacy and Higher Education," from *Journal of Academic Librarianship*. This article was written as a response to another article discussing the theme of how to increase the information literacy of college undergraduate students. Zabel agrees with the author of the other article that the cost of information illiteracy is too great to ignore. Without information literacy, too many people are willing to accept thinly disguised marketing schemes as fact. He disagrees, however, with the other author who claims that the best way to increase information literacy in undergraduates is to require them to take an information literacy class. Zabel counters this with the arguments about the cost of college already being too high and the lack of evidence that such a course actually increases student informational literacy. Zabel also points out an alternative which is based on public school successes integrating informational literacy into core courses. He postulates that what is needed is for librarians to work with the instructors to weave information literacy into the curricula by requiring that students do actual research as a part of the course. Thus, instructors fortify their curriculum and increase the rigor and the effectual learning of each of their students.

of the library because their coursework does not require them to do so. This is a critical issue" (2004, p. 19). Especially in high school, but also starting early in students' academic careers, teachers must require students to do research. If teachers would take advantage of not only the abundant content knowledge available in their libraries and through electronic resources, but also the pedagogical research available, then they would be more capable of adjusting to the needs of the new types of students who walk through their doors. In addition, teachers would be able to enjoy more success in their instruction.

One way to promote active learning is to not only look at data from the United States, but also to research other countries, as suggested by Lauer and Yodanis (2004). These scholars use qualitative data from an internationally-administered survey to illustrate sociological differences between countries and to increase the value and relevance of their instruction. And, more importantly, they provide a foundation of inquiry for students to discover what the data suggests about different cultures and practices across the world (Lauer & Yodanis, 2004). "Many teachers also find that the infusion of data analysis increases active learning across the curriculum" (Lauer & Yodanis, 2004, p. 305). This active learning is what all teachers should strive for. A teacher who regularly employs this sort of scholarly research in instruction will also be modeling the same behaviors expected of students.

Finally, teachers must reject the traditions of isolation and become instructional leaders of their students and of their peers. In public schools, this mean that these inspired teachers must actively work to establish learning communities, which are composed of small groups of their peers united in purpose. According to Rick DuFour and Robert Eaker (1998), these teacher learning teams must agree to identify specific student needs, research possible solutions, perform action research, gather data on results, and analyze them in order to be truly effective.

As a member of a learning team, such a teacher will share the gems of knowledge gained from staying abreast of research-based practices, push for higher standards as a practitioner, and model accountability for student performance results as an instructional leader. The motivation for doing all this will come from expectations and interactions of the other teachers in the group. As a member of a teacher learning team, every teacher will be expected to be a scholar and analyze student data and research educational solutions to the findings. Each teacher will be a practitioner in implementing the agreed upon research-based strategy and in evaluating the effectiveness on student learning. Finally, each teacher will have to be an instructional leader in the teacher learning community in order to have the courage to do what is best for students and not simply convenient for teachers. The Wright State Teacher Leadership

Program recognizes this critical need and has created a program that trains teachers to be "teacher leaders" of students and their peers. "The content embedded within the Wright State Teacher Leadership Program reflects the belief that teacher leadership is the cornerstone for both effective building leadership and classroom teaching" (Hambright & Franco, 2008, p. 17).

Today, teachers must be scholars, practitioners, and leaders in order to meet the needs of students in today's classrooms. They also need to be informationally literate so they never isolate themselves from professional development when they enter their classrooms and close their doors.

Helping Students Become Informationally Literate

Because students have changed so much and every group of students has different needs, teachers must be able to adapt and adjust their instruction accordingly. This cannot be accomplished if teachers have succumbed to the negative effects of isolation. Physical isolation brings about a worse isolation problem: informational isolation. Teachers suffering from this do not stay abreast of their professional research and find it difficult to deal with today's students. In order to combat this, each teacher must become informationally literate. Informational literacy will allow teachers to become model scholars for their students, effective practitioners of sound pedagogy, and influential leaders of their peers and the students they teach.

> *"I have never let my schooling get in the way of my education."*
>
> MARK TWAIN

How to Help Students Be Good Information Gatherers

Scholarly writing is different from other writing because of the audience that will be reading it. Accepted norms must be followed, evidence and research must be included, and ideas must flow in a logical manner to a concrete conclusion. Scholarly writing has two purposes: to increase the understanding of the reader and to increase the understanding of the author.

Scholarly writing is more than simple communication. Davies (2000) makes the distinction that there are two types of writing: that which does not require composing, such as forms and surveys, and that which does, such as scholarly writing (p. 434). Scholarly writing's purpose is to lay out the facts and the evidence, organize them, and make sense of them. Scholarly writing can manifest itself in many formats, disciplines, and media, but in every case, the author establishes an opinion and offers supporting evidence in an attempt to convince others to think the same way. The stronger the evidence, the easier it is to persuade others. The CCSS would maintain that argument is more powerful than mere persuasion.

One might ask how students might gain understanding from the act of scholarly writing. First of all, scholarly writing is difficult. Davies (2000) quotes research indicating that the mental capacity to produce scholarly writing approaches "OVERLOADING" (p. 436). The mental exercise of writing serves as a tool to refine and deepen thinking. According to Davies (2000), writing is the most important invention humans ever made because it helps them think—even surpassing the computer (p. 436). All the components of scholarly writing—investigation, building an argument, accuracy, peer review, and evidence—help achieve the purpose of making the reader think critically and the writer think more profoundly. Writing thoughts on paper raises the level of importance and trust in those thoughts; therefore, the accuracy and the quality of the writing must be increased too (Davies, 2000, p. 436).

Because it is a beneficial exercise for both the reader and the writer, scholarly writing should be done more often in the classroom. Why don't teachers use research and scholarly writing? Williams and Coles (2007) discovered that teachers say they do not use research because of lack of time and lack of availability of sources. Yet in reality, when questioned about their comfort level, teachers felt they were less comfortable using research because they felt they were less capable of utilizing research information than general knowledge information. In other words, they were lacking in information literacy skills. One of the first jobs of a teacher would be to help all students become information literate.

Another reason that teachers may not be using research information is the perception that it is not applicable to their classrooms. In fact, Miller, Drill, and Behrstock (2010) indicate that teachers categorize their use of research into three different categories: "localized learning, easily accessible formats, and how they can apply the research to a local context" (p. 32).

In reality, the only way to actually get students to base their learning decisions on sound research is to not accept *any* decisions that are not based on sound research. In other words, the teacher will always ask students, "Show me the research that you have done on this topic that supports your decision." If no research is done, then the discussion is over, and no decision will be made. If the research is from a salesman, is shoddy, or comes from Wikipedia, then the answer will be the same. Students need to learn that the validity of the sources of the information is more important than the research itself.

As educational leaders, teachers must, of course, set the example of effective research skills for their students. If we are requiring students to cite sources and find and list references, then in the documents that we give the students, those same elements must exist. Students will need direct instruction on how to do research. If you are rusty about your own research skills, you can work with your librarian. If you are not an English teacher, you can ask the English department to help you train your students to perform research, validate sources, use primary and secondary sources, and use APA, MLA, or Chicago style. All the help you could want for your students to become college-ready researchers is at your fingertips. When searching for APA format help on the computer, Purdue University is the first site that appears and is full of helpful explanations, examples, and tips for doing research.

Student scholarly writing is so important that the College Board is doing a pilot program unofficially called the Capstone Project. They noticed that students graduate from high school with a jumble of disparate AP courses under their belts, and aside from similar AP strategies used in some courses, there really is no unifying thread tying them all together and making students "college-ready." Under the direction of Ariel Foster, Executive Director, College and University Services Advanced Placement Program, the College Board is proposing that high schools offer the AP | Cambridge Capstone Program and Credential, which consists of two courses taken during junior and senior year. In the junior-year course, students will learn to refine their college-readiness skills in analysis, critical thinking, and problem solving. Their senior year, students will engage in a full-blown, 20-page research project. Students then graduate with an AP credential, not just potential college credit. Since it is a pilot program, colleges are still unsure of what kind of college credit, if any, will be given for these two courses. Both of these courses compose a unifying experience for students, an experience that serves as a capstone to the hard-learned lessons from having taken multiple AP courses. This pilot program is slated to be tested in 2012–2014, principally in the burgeoning school districts of Dade County, Florida.[42]

---

[42]Four Miami-Dade County public high schools were initially selected for inclusion in the capstone pilot project out of a total of 15 to 18 schools worldwide. This program is supported by some heavy hitters, such as MIT, the University of Washington, and Florida State University. You can read more about it at http://press.collegeboard.org/releases/2012/college-board-and-university-cambridge-international-examinations-announce-new-education-pro

There is a growing body of evidence supporting scholarly writing in high school and its effect on preparing students to be successful in college, including vocabulary development and critical thinking skills (Schroeder, 2006; Wolsey, 2010; Peters, 2011; Jones, 2012). Because writing is an "active" learning process, it requires students to utilize all of the thinking skills: analytical, critical, and creative. It only stands to reason that the more students write, the better they get at thinking. And as I have reminded you before, thinking enhances . . . yes, that is right—memory!

S T R A T E G Y

Test It Out

Students can certainly obtain mountains of research for their scholarly writing from Internet sources, libraries, and teachers, but especially in science and math classes, it is advantageous for students to acquire their own data. They can do this by creating surveys, taking measurements, and testing hypotheses. Under your guidance, students can use this newly-created data to write scholarly works of real relevance and interest to them. Following are some ideas on how this might work.

TECHNIQUE: Pilot. Students can perform pilot tests of their ideas. As with any "test," the data obtained from the pilot serves as the basis for scholarly writing, including argument or persuasive essays.

TECHNIQUE: Dry run. Students can walk through full implementation of their ideas before implementing them. This is similar to the "what if" scenarios often assigned to students. Being able to think through the most likely results of a hypothesis, theory, or course of action and map them out in narrative form is a valuable higher-order thinking skill.

TECHNIQUE: Dress rehearsal. Students can practice the data-gathering exercise with all the actors in place. Such collaborative learning assumes that many times the answers are not available and must be arrived at through intense group interaction, conversation, debate, argument, and persuasion. Students can play their roles as if they are actually in the situation, and as a result will be able to see possible realities in the consequences as the interaction unfolds.

TECHNIQUE: Slice of pie data slice. Take one day in the life of the protagonist and gather data on what is learned, accomplished, set in motion, etc. One of the most intriguing movies I have seen is called *Rosencrantz and Gildenstern Are Dead.* It takes two insignificant characters from the Shakespearian play *Hamlet* and tells their story as the play unfolds around them. In a humorous way, it also illustrates the gaps of information about purpose that these two characters experience.[43] Using their imaginations, students can do a similar analysis by following the protagonist of a literary work as they perform their roles in the course of a day. Students may discover reasons that the author might have left out details, or that particular details were included that would otherwise be overlooked in a typical literary analysis.

TECHNIQUE: Simulation. Without actually performing the experiment, students will test their hypothesis as a simulated experiment. For example, the NASA.gov website is full of simulations upon which students can test their hypothesis. One of the favorite simulations is the water-bottle rocket. NASA has a program in which students can manipulate variables such as size of the rocket, amount of water placed in the rocket, amount of air pressure, wind, atmospheric humidity, temperature, etc. Then students can hit the fire button and view the simulated results. Next, students can create a rocket and following the simulation, attempt to produce the same results out in the field.

---

[43] Gary Oldman, Timm Ross, and Richard Dreyfuss star in *Rosencrantz and Guildenstern Are Dead*, written and directed by Tom Stoppard in 1990. Just a warning about this film: it is much more enjoyable after studying *Hamlet* because the humor and the scenes are all dependent upon the actual play that unfolds around Rosencrantz and Guildenstern as they perform their scripted lines, and curiously react to the play in the gaps between. More information about this creative movie can be found at www.imdb.com/title/tt0100519

Chapter 12

Drawing Inferences and Reaching Conclusions

To infer and conclude: Derive understanding and meaning from what is and is not stated

Why Do Students Need to Be Skilled at Drawing Inferences and Reaching Conclusions?

The CCSS place a great value on the ability of students to draw inferences and reach conclusions. In fact, the College and Career Readiness Anchor Standards for Reading establish the importance of drawing inferences in the first standard: Key Ideas and Details (see Figure 12.1).

Drawing inferences has a lot to do with simply looking at words. Let's look first at the word "drawing." Though the word has several different meanings, only one is most applicable to this situation. The word *drawing* in terms of creating a work of art with a piece of charcoal or graphite doesn't seem to fit, primarily because it includes the creation of, or fabrication of, or re-creation of something on a blank medium that was not there before. When an artist is drawing in this manner, there is the idea of interpretation and conveyance of meaning from which the artist derives certain liberties to be able to change or alter reality in order to communicate some message to the viewer. Comparatively, it is said that the best authors are able to communicate with words what artists are able to communicate with paint, charcoal,

Figure 12.1 CCSS Reading Anchor Standard: Key Ideas and Details

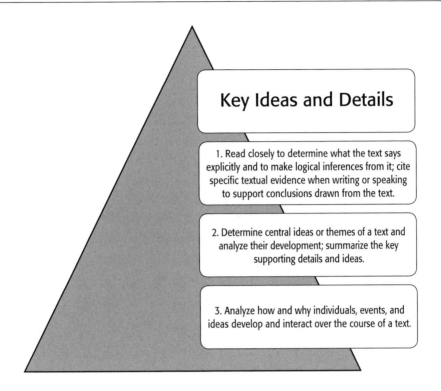

Key Ideas and Details

1. Read closely to determine what the text says explicitly and to make logical inferences from it; cite specific textual evidence when writing or speaking to support conclusions drawn from the text.

2. Determine central ideas or themes of a text and analyze their development; summarize the key supporting details and ideas.

3. Analyze how and why individuals, events, and ideas develop and interact over the course of a text.

and pencil (though it takes at least one thousand of them). But this isn't what I would like to understand from the word *drawing* as in drawing inferences, because that would put the artist in the same category as the writer, which are primary roles, when in fact the act of drawing inferences lies within the realm of the literate reader or art aficionado—a secondary role, more of interpretation than creation.

Another definition of *draw* refers to the act of pulling a cart with a horse, or raising water out of a well. It is a transitive verb, meaning that you must draw something; the action of drawing transfers to an object, like water. If we think of the phrase, "draw water out of a well," then this form of the word *draw* would seem to indicate pulling something out of something else. I believe that we are getting close here. We need to look more closely at the word *infer* again. I always confuse the words *infer* and *imply*. Though they mean the same thing, one of them is used by the creator of a communication, while the other is used by the receiver of that communication. If the implication is the message that is intended to be sent, that would mean that the inference is the interpretation of the implication. Okay, that's it. Now we are ready for a conclusion to be made. Hmp, hmp, hmpmm (clearing one's throat) . . . A college-ready reader is able to pull intended meaning from within a text as easily and as effectively as a maiden would draw water from a well.

There you have it: a moderately succinct analysis of the meanings of the words *draw, infer,* and *imply.* The reason a college-ready reader, observer, or listener would want to draw inferences is because no author, actor, or orator writes, portrays, or says anything that does not have at least two levels of meaning. By level of meaning I refer to at least the actual meaning and the figurative meaning. It takes no great skill to interpret the actual meaning, but it takes a literate mind to be able to infer a more figurative meaning or holistic meaning. This begins with asking the question, "Why would an author write a prose in the first place?" That would be the first message that can be inferred from any text. Writing is not easy and requires significant motivation to complete. It helps to know something about the author and the environment in which the prose was written. Many times the author will intentionally or unintentionally assist the reader in this regard. Other "why" questions must follow: Why does the author use a certain style of writing? Why does the protagonist use a certain language? After asking particular questions like these, the college-ready reader will be able to begin to draw inferences from the reading as to what larger messages the author wishes to convey to the reading audience.

College- and career-ready students are able to read complex texts and draw inferences and conclusions by using analysis skills as discussed in chapter one, by using critical thinking skills as described in chapter two, and by using the creative thinking skills described in chapter three to put them all together to form a final message.

How to Help Students to Succeed in Drawing Inferences and Reaching Conclusions

In this chapter, I would like to model for you a possible interpretation of a piece of literature so that you can see for yourself what kind of thinking college- and career-ready students need to be prepared to do. My example is only one interpretation, but as we learned earlier from the CCSS College and Career Readiness Anchor Standards for Reading, it is not enough to simply draw logical inferences. Students must also be able to substantiate their interpretations with evidence from literature.

For example, on the surface, John Steinbeck's *The Pearl* tells a story of a poor family that happens upon what some would consider significant wealth: a large pearl. Through a series of unfortunate events, the family comes to the conclusion that to find peace, the pearl must be thrown back into the sea. However, the reader can infer many other messages: Humanity is essentially selfish and greedy. Wealth is considered to bring happiness and contentment. Desperation motivates horrible acts of cruelty. Each of these inferences is exposed as if a search light shone upon it in the different scenes of the story. The conclusion that is to be reached can only be arrived at by understanding these intermediate inferred messages and then combining them into a whole.

On the surface, one might consider the story a message of futility in which the latter state of Juana and Kino was worse than the initial state. Another conclusion beckons our attention, however. A transformation has occurred. Juana and Kino began in innocence, living peacefully, but over the course of the story, their original view of friendship and their trust of humanity were altered. Then, as a response to their own reactions to the pearl, they were forced to leave behind their former life. When the trackers relentlessly followed them, their feelings of self-protection changed to anger and revenge. The final return to the sea to dispose of the pearl was not an absolution of guilt, but a final turning point in the transformation from blissful ignorance of innocence to wretched wisdom of experience. The Juana and Kino standing on the beach were not the same Juana and Kino who had originally found the pearl. A possible message to be concluded from Steinbeck's writing is that life brings us pearls and sorrows, but wisdom is the final pearl.

In my Philosophy 110 critical thinking class, one of the assignments for beginning college students is to analyze a speech from a movie to help prepare to present a convincing argument. There is a great website that you will also want to consider: *www.americanrhetoric.com.* To show my students an example of how to do the analysis, I tried to pull up the speech from the section on movie speeches. I had originally chosen a speech labeled as one delivered by Captain Kirk of *Star Trek.* When I clicked on the link, it turned out to be only the introductory words spoken at the beginning of each episode: "Our five year mission. . . ." That was too simple, I thought, so I chose a speech from the movie *A Perfect Storm.* When it came time to discuss this in the lesson, that particular speech would not load due to technical difficulties. "Well," I thought, "I know that the *Star Trek* theme will load, and I might as well do a simple analysis for time's sake." So that is what I did. Figure 12.2 shows the words of the opening screens of the 1960s *Star Trek* program as the spaceship swooshes by (I never understood how that could happen in the vacuum of space, anyway).

Figure 12.2 Analysis of the *Star Trek* Theme (Photographs courtesy of NASA Hubble Space Telescope)

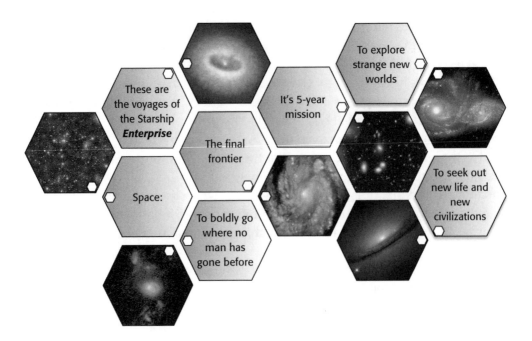

Following are some of the questions that came up in our discussion. I was surprised that such a small text could bring out so much. Drawing inferences and reaching conclusions includes making some assumptions. A logical assumption then is that in the future depicted by Star Trek, man has conquered all frontiers except space. That makes me think about our current situation. If space in the future is the final frontier, what is our current frontier? What frontiers have been conquered already? What frontiers will need to be conquered to arrive at the "final frontier"? Going on to the rest of the monologue, Why five years and not ten or three? What is significant about five? What is the definition of strange? To seek out new life and civilizations is a good goal, but what will happen when they are found? How do they know that no man has gone before? We thought originally that Columbus was the first to visit the Americas, but it turns out the Vikings had been there earlier. What is meant by the word *man*?

The goal is to get students to ask these kinds of questions, to analyze the literature or text, to think about it critically, and then to think creatively in order to come up with logical conclusions about the meanings that can be inferred. Following are strategies and the associated techniques that can help you do this.

S T R A T E G Y

Issues Versus Problems

Problems are situations, events, or states of being that need to be solved. They simply need to be fixed. Issues, on the other hand, need to be fixed, but people do not agree on how to do it. Issues have more than one perspective for interpretation and for this reason are controversial. For example, "Students dropping out of high school" is a problem. Everyone agrees that it needs to be fixed. "High schools cause students to drop out" is a controversial issue, and there are multiple ways to interpret this statement.

S T R A T E G Y

Convergent and Divergent Thinking

In terms of computer information systems, knowledge is power. Innovative companies understand that their innovators need knowledge in order to combine into new things. Even more important is the combination of knowledge from different parts of the company. Companies go to great lengths to make sure that the people in their companies have access to this knowledge. When knowledge from different disciplines is combined, it is convergent, but when new ideas and products are formed, these are divergent from the norm.[44]

---

[44] You can read about creativity and how knowledge both enhances divergent thinking and inhibits it in this interesting report. Müller-Wienbergen, F., Müller, O., Seidel, S., & Becker, J. (2011). Leaving the Beaten Tracks in Creative Work - A Design Theory for Systems that Support Convergent and Divergent Thinking. *Journal of the Association for Information Systems, 12*(11), 714-740. Retrieved March 29, 2012, from https://search.ebscohost.com/login.aspx?direct=true&db=bth&AN=71702708&site=eds-live

TECHNIQUE: *Convergence.* In groups, students practice convergence by categorizing themes or topics from various works of literature they have read into a single unifying list. The teacher provides the topic of "Finding something that was lost." Students may combine Lewis Carroll's *Alice's Adventures in Wonderland*, Frances Hodgson Burnett's *The Secret Garden*, and Walter Farley's *The Black Stallion* with Antoine de Saint-Exupéry's *The Little Prince*,[45] all under the category of finding something that was lost. For the divergent thinking part of this exercise, students must then take parts from each story and find at least three new themes. For example, each story has elements of personal journey, each story depends on an intimately childish perspective, and each story is a story of escape.

S T R A T E G Y

Inductive and Deductive Reasoning

Dictionaries do not agree on what deductive and inductive reasoning are. Some say that deductive goes from general to specific and inductive from specific to general. Other dictionaries say that deduction establishes irrefutable facts, while induction deals only with most likely probabilities. Some definitions state that deduction deals with rules while induction deals with experiences. It really doesn't matter whether something is solved inductively or deductively, as long as it is solved. Both inductive and deductive thinking require that the facts be analyzed. Making the correct connections between the disparate facts makes solving the problem, as Holmes would put it, "elementary." A deducted conclusion is not plainly stated but rather sits between facts. For our purposes, we will take deductive reasoning to mean concerned with concrete facts, and inductive to mean concerned with high degrees of probability.

TECHNIQUE: *Inference.* Provide for students a selection in which the situation must be inferred rather than explained. Have students work in pairs to deduce a conclusion from the relevant facts. An example is in Figure 12.3.

---

[45] All of these books come from the CCSS ELA Appendix B reading list for fourth and fifth grades (CCSSI, 2010d, p. 7).

Figure 12.3 Example of Inference

Singer, Isaac Bashevis. "Zlateh the Goat." *Zlateh the Goat and Other Stories.* New York: HarperCollins, 2001. (1984)

"The snow fell for three days, though after the first day it was not as thick and the wind quieted down. Sometimes Aaron felt that there could never have been a summer, that the snow had always fallen, ever since he could remember. He, Aaron, never had a father or mother or sisters. He was a snow child, born of the snow, and so was Zlateh. It was so quiet in the hay that his ears rang in the stillness. Aaron and Zlateh slept all night and a good part of the day. As for Aaron's dreams, they were all about warm weather. He dreamed of green fields, trees covered with blossoms, clear brooks, and singing birds. By the third night the snow had stopped, but Aaron did not dare to find his way home in the darkness. The sky became clear and the moon shone, casting silvery nets on the snow. Aaron dug his way out and looked at the world. It was all white, quiet, dreaming dreams of heavenly splendor. The stars were large and close. The moon swam in the sky as in a sea" (CCSSI, 2010d, p. 64).

Deductive Questions to Answer: (Concrete Facts)	**Inductive Questions to Answer: (Probability)**
Where is the story taking place? What season is it? What do we know about the characters? Who is Zlateh?	What does the character want? How did the characters get there? What is the character's relationship with snow?

Conclusion: Aaron and the Goat stay in a hay stack to survive a blizzard. For Aaron this is part of the life he accepts as a "snow child." His goal is to return home safely.

Chapter
13

Uses Technology as a Tool,
Not a Crutch

Technology: A tool to think with

Why Is It Critical for Students to
Use Technology To Learn?

So far technology has changed K–12 education in two ways: how information is obtained and how it is shared. Even with advances in technology, the actual act of teaching remains generally unchanged, regardless of the technology available in the classroom. Some teachers have adopted PowerPoint lectures, and LCD projectors have replaced overhead projectors. Some have even begun using SMART Boards as a method of instruction. But teachers for the most part stand in front of the class and talk to students. There is good and bad to that, but my point is that in order for technology to really affect student learning, teaching has to change. The new technology needs to be in the hands of the students. In addition, teachers have to be able to design learning environments that promote student-directed learning more than teacher-directed learning. It doesn't matter what the "teacher" is doing if students are not learning. In essence, what we consider "teaching" has to be minimized, and the focus has to shift to "learning." Computers and other devices can help a lot here.

The biggest change in education has occurred in learning in and especially out of the classroom. Computers have changed how students are able to learn.

Way back in the 80s when Seymour Papert was touting the kid-friendly computer programming language called Logo as the way students would learn best, we knew that technology could help students explore their world. (That was before the Internet.) The vision then, and now, was to use computers to improve learning. Computers have been time-saving devices and effective communication tools, but too often we forget that they can't do everything. (How many SMART Boards are simply used as projection screens or whiteboards?) I can envision the day that the technology fades into the scenery, and rather than being on the center stage, as it is now, it becomes simply an everyday tool to "think with."

Because of modern computers and the Internet, the acquisition of knowledge does not have to be sequential or synchronous, because students can, and do, find information according to their interests because of Wiki, Google, or Jeeves. The time it takes to research something is drastically reduced compared to taking a trip to the library. This has brought other issues to the forefront—plagiarism, individual thinking, creativity, etc. Students do not have to trust the teacher or the textbook—they can find out for themselves both sides of any argument. Students do not have to create in a linear fashion either. With computers, students can write a report, jumble it around, add, delete, etc., all without onion-skin paper, erasures, or correcting tape. The end result is that modern students do not have to "think" in a linear or compartmentalized fashion, which more closely matches the physiology of the brain.

The thing about our learning organ or brain is that it is not just in our skull. It incorporates (good word) our whole body. It is not necessary that we teach one or the other of the multiple intelligences. Every student has all of the "intelligences" but may prefer using some rather than others. It is the job of a good teacher to incorporate as many "intelligences" as possible into the learning, especially the bodily-kinesthetic elements. This is to get learning started. A good teacher will help students develop the "other" intelligences. The accelerometer in the iPad and iPod have interesting possibilities. Stride, balance, force, acceleration, and rhythm can now be part of "academic" intelligence learning. These apps have not been invented yet, nor have the rubber enclosures to protect and utilize the iPad/iPod. But it won't be long until they are invented.

I think the next obvious step in education technology was just taken by Apple, through etext books on the iPad with apps for people to write multimedia textbooks. This YouTube video describes what Apple has done to radically improve the way students and teachers interact with textbooks: *www.youtube.com/watch?v=443zQOLHNk*. With this, there is no reason that the iPad will not hasten the long-awaited demise of the textbook. Everything that students need will be right there at the touch of a finger.

But we have a long way to go before technology becomes as ubiquitous as the pencil in helping students think better. I think perhaps the best vision of the future I have seen is the Corning glass YouTube video, "A Day Made of Glass. . . ." *www.youtube.com/watch?v=6Cf7IL_eZ38*. So iPads are a step in the right direction as an information-gathering, presenting, and organizing tool, but they are not so hot at creating (though that might change soon, especially as we see voice-activated technologies increase their accuracy and utility).

If I had thirty iPads in my class, what would I do with them? How would I use them to help students learn better and help me teach better? Perhaps a better question is this: What would I do with them that I could not do with other tools that are available and are cheaper? Certainly iPads are cheaper than computers (desktops or laptops), and they are more mobile. Speaking of computers, they were supposed to be the transformation of teaching and learning as we know it. In some ways there has been a transformation, but the basics of teaching and learning have remained unchanged. Perhaps the iPad will be the tool that really does transform teaching and learning. In the next section, I discuss some of the unique features of the iPad and the free apps that take advantage of them. Enjoy!

The iPad has a number of unique features that provide for interesting possibilities in teaching and learning. The motion sensor of the iPad has a number of intriguing applications for learning. Most students today would be classified as bodily-kinesthetic learners. The motion sensor allows students to use their hands in guiding the iPad to equilibrium, balance skills, or remote control of real or virtual robotics, hovercraft, or other vehicles. Students can use the Clineometer app to measure the level of a wall or surface, and also the precise angles of incline or decline. With the internal accelerometers in the iPad, physics experiments of acceleration or change in force can be measured. Imagine taking the iPad with you on a roller coaster ride. Imagine calculating angles and force and then shooting odd birds from a slingshot, destroying buildings and colliding with green pig heads (ever heard of Angry Birds?). Rubberized iPads and iPods in gym class can measure levels of exertion, balance, and repetitions.

As a completely portable learning tool, the iPad camera allows documentation to be taken to a whole different level. An app called Field Notes LT not only allows students to take copious notes of their observations, but it also attaches the date, time, GPS location, and photographs of what is observed. These notes can be instantly shared, used in collaborations, and published in the field. Students can also attach videos and voice recordings to their field notes. Students can dictate to the iPad using the Dragon Dictation app, and it will type their words. With iPads in the same network but in different locations, using the Assemblee app, students can create a collaboration web to share findings and discuss conclusions about different perspectives of the same project.

In math class, the GPS of the iPad establishes locale in profound ways. Students can use the included Map app to calculate distances, compare routes, and determine actual speeds of the westbound and the eastbound trains common in word problems. The mathematics involved with trip-planning and decision-making are brought to life with actual, real-time photographs, maps, and weather data provided by the Google Earth app, Big Blue Marble HD, and many others. The app called TourWrist allows students 360 degree views, "tours" of locations of interest throughout the world. With DerManDar, students can take their own 360-degree pictures of places they visit.

Of course, the mobility provided by the iPad's wireless telephone connection capability allows unprecedented access to the Internet anywhere students are. This is truly information on demand. As questions arise, students can "Google" for clues and insights to begin their studies. Even more powerfully, though, through the iPad phone connection, students can have access to volumes of "primary source" documents and data to help with their investigations in or out of the classroom, on the bus, in a restaurant, or at a football game.

Because iPads do not have USB ports, disk drives, or CDROM/DVD capability, methods for sharing data with other computers and devices over the Internet or "cloud" have been developed. Dropbox allows students to set up a personal account in which they can store iPad-created documents, photos, fieldnotes, etc, and they can access those documents from any other computer or Internet-capable device. Evernote helps students keep track of their notes, and Mendeley organizes research documents and lets students take the research they've done on their computers with them whereever they are going. Project Gutenberg allows students to download thousands of classic books to be read on any number of free book-reader apps available.With the HMH Fuse app, students have at their fingertips the entire Houghton-Mifflin *Algebra 1* book along with exercises and tools for learning algebra.

Teachers can give presentations while walking around the classroom and interacting with students, by controlling their own computers from their iPads with the Remote Mouse app. With a simple cable, teachers can use their iPads to present their unique and creative Prezi presentations made on their computers by using the iPad application called Prezi Player. The teacher can control the document by simply pinching, twisting, and sliding their fingers across the face of the iPad.

Aside from finding the gazillions of games, tutoring programs, and pointless apps available for free, a diligent teacher can find treasures of apps for their iPads that engage and challenge student minds in creative ways. Some of my favorites are Lasers Free, Trainyard EX, Play Chess, Words with Friends HD, and Contre Jour (not free but worth the $1.99).

How to Help Students Enhance Learning with Technology

Okay, I will admit it. I am addicted to technology. I cannot add two and two . . . well I can, but I prefer to use the calculator, spreadsheet, or computer calculator to do it for me. I find writing long hand ponderous (or onerous). I tend to write and then rewrite and then add and then delete and then revise and then write some more. My thinking isn't sequential, so it is confining to have to write that way. I was drawn to computers early on, but in my high school days, computers were novel toys, and not until college did the advent of Word Perfect allow them to be used as word processors. It was at this point that I began my real dependence on computers as "tools to think with" and "tools to create with."

The one thing I do prefer to do without technology is read (though the Kindle and other eReaders are so like books, it is scary). Even still, I prefer to read real books and magazines because I can mark the pages, make notes, put tabs in them, and dog-ear the corners. There is another reason—and iPads and other eReaders have addressed this to a point—which is that information in a book or magazine has a location, a physical page. I can remember what side of the page a quote is on a book or magazine, but if it is a continuous stream of words, there is no locale memory. I must admit, however, that when I am using Adobe Reader, the search tool is very handy when looking for information—but this can also be a crutch because if I can find what I want, I tend to skip reading the whole book and end up reading only a part of it. I, and many desperate teenagers trying to write reports, have found that copy and paste is a great feature (crutch) of electronic media when you are short on time (of course I/we cite sources, but why retype them if you don't have to?).

The very real danger with the ease of use and open access to the Internet is that students will spend their time browsing, copying, and adapting the work of others, rather than analyzing, criticizing, or creating their own work. Dependent behaviors such as these cripple student creativity and serve as a crutch to mediocrity. With or without technology, those thinking skills require effort and an expenditure of willpower and determination to understand, judge, and create. The ability to communicate cannot be replaced by technology, just as a poor speaker cannot hope to cover that up by using PowerPoint. But a great communicator uses technology to enhance an already powerful message and its delivery.

We have already learned that writing is a way to clarify and refine thinking. Technology tools make that process a lot easier. Mind mapping software such as Inspiration and the freeware Freeminds are tools to help students organize their thoughts visually. Making those explicit connections using bubbles and arrows is an excellent way to clarify thinking, spot gaps in thinking, and establish new routes for thinking. Inspiration can take the creation of mind maps one step further. By adding visual imagery for each concept in addition to the words, such mind maps would access additional attention to detail and serve as a non-linguistic representation to aid memory. For some, simply using the Microsoft suite of programs is plenty to manipulate information, present information, evaluate information, and create. We can at least start preparing our students to be college-ready and especially career-ready by helping them master these tools.

In the completion of my doctorate, and doing research for this book, I depended on Zotero to keep all of my research sources straight, and I used Mendeley and Dropbox to share my library among computers. I was able to not only keep track of all of the hundreds of resources used, but also categorize them and cross-reference them. One of the features that was most useful is the search feature. I might be able to remember a few key words or the author of the research. All I have to do is a simple search of my database, and I can usually find what I am looking for. I can't tell you how much time this saves me. I can't imagine doing research without these tools. Students whom we are trying to prepare to be college- and career-ready should have access to similar tools and should be taught how to use them. Gathering research is hard enough as it is, but evaluating the validity of the resource is another. It is also something that technology cannot do. The CCSS require students to distinguish the value of sources—wiki vs real research. While general Google searches may be useful and allow students to get basic knowledge, students need to know how to then to dig deeper into the subject. Students need to know how to validate sources by checking facts and looking up references. Students need to know how to validate data by triangulation with at least two other sources of data. Students need to know how to read research and extract valuable information to support thesis statements. The best way for students to learn these research skills is to require them to use them.

Students and teachers who are a little more computer confident have found that ample supplies of "open-source" software exist to meet just about every computer need you might have. So that is the key—computer confidence. Can we say that anymore these days? Technology is so much more than "computers" now. My phone has more computing power and memory than my first laptop, but I am from the older generation that is still surprised by this. Our students have grown up in a world where technology has abounded. I frequently learn from my son as he figures out things to do on his cell phone, iPod, and computers. It would be presumptuous of us to try to show teenagers anything about technology that they do not already know. Our role in helping students use technology to prepare them to be college- and career-ready is to require them to use these tech tools in the learning that goes on in our classrooms. The strategy and the techniques that follow are based on that principle.

S T R A T E G Y

Coloring Book with No Lines

In the past, teachers were intent on uniformity and obedience to demonstrate effective learning. It was the height of effrontery to color outside of the lines. We still hear that phrase today as a challenge to think creatively and ignore the normal constraints imposed in regular public education. Now, through the magic of technology, we have the capacity to give students a true coloring book with no lines. The sky is the limit in terms of what students can create, and "no lines" refers to eliminating the control of a teacher. Following are open-ended software tools that students can use to create and to communicate. The best strategy in these situations is to show students what the program is and then get out of their way and let them show you how to make it sing (figuratively of course).

♦ HyperStudio, written by former science teacher Roger Wagner, is a multimedia presentation tool powerful enough for advanced high school students and intuitive enough for elementary students. You (your students) can find out more about HyperStudio at *www.mackiev. com/hyperstudio/index.html*

♦ Prezi is an intriguing presentation tool with a free version for educators. The program allows presentations to be formed by imbedding smaller and smaller images into the drawing frame. As the presenter clicks on the presentation, the images are magnified, revealing a new perspective that was there all along but was just too small to see. The conceptual connection of identifying smaller related elements of a larger picture are profound and highly interesting. You (your students) can learn more about this program at *www.prezi.com*

SECTION IV
CONCLUSION

Creating Effective Communicators

An effective communicator reaches out to his audience, touches their hearts, and animates their brains in writing and in the spoken word. An effective communicator creates a common understanding by choosing powerful vocabulary to convey powerful meaning. The future of our society depends on students leaving our schools as college-ready communicators. Today communication is instantaneous, and so is miscommunication. Once an electronic message has gone out, it is very difficult to retrieve it from the four corners of the earth. Even still, technology enhances communication more than it disables it.

For example, the California condor is one of the most efficient travelers. It can glide for hours with only a twitch of its tail. Students using technology gain the same kind of efficiency with a few clicks of a mouse. My vision of the future of education and technology in the next five years includes some of the following:

♦ Breakthroughs in batteries will allow the iPads and phones to get thinner with larger screens. The plethora of tablets, eReaders, and phones will become more ubiquitous (ya gotta love that word). More and more textbooks will follow the lead of Apple and others and become interactive.

♦ Integrated technology will become even more widespread. Similar to what computers did for cars, we will see auto-sync technology with integrated technology in shoes, belt buckles, pens and pencils, rings, earrings (blueteeth?), and virtual displays included in fashion sunglasses and prescription eyewear (*Mission Impossible*-type contact lenses?).

The bottom line question that we need to ask is, "How can I employ all of this to help get students college- and career-ready?"

FINAL NOTES

Effective communication is dependent on knowledge gained through effective research. Effective research depends on diligent scholarship of well-trained minds. Developing these incredibly important habits of mind depends on large quantities of practice in thinking analytically, thinking critically, and thinking creatively.

It is my hope that you, as a teacher or practitioner of learning, have gained a higher vision of your calling as an educator, and that you will use this book to be able to look beyond the minimum standards imposed by the states and the federal government and establish the ten mental habits that I shared with you as the bulwark of your instructional efforts.

1. Analytic Thinkers (this is thinking about the parts and pieces of the whole)
2. Critical Thinkers (this is thinking about effectiveness and validity)
3. Problem Solvers (this is more than a one size fits all heuristic)
4. Inquisitive Nature (this is curiosity on steroids)
5. Opportunistic (takes advantage of learning opportunities—learns now rather than later)
6. Flexible (ability and desire to cope with frustration and ambiguity)
7. Open-Minded (willingness to accept critical feedback)
8. Teachable (willingness to adjust based on feedback)
9. Risk Takers (openness to possible failure)
10. Expressive (ability to communicate in writing and orally)

The Common Core State Standards are a boon to help us because they are founded on these characteristics. Because the CCSS simplify what to teach, we can focus more on the how to teach it and be more effective at inspiring learning in our students.

REFERENCES

Albergaria Almeida, P. (2010). Questioning Patterns, Questioning Profiles and Teaching Strategies in Secondary Education. *International Journal of Learning*, 17(1), 587–600. *doi:10.1504/IJLC.2010.035833*

American College Testing Program, I. A. (2006). Reading between the lines: What the ACT reveals about college readiness in reading. *American College Testing (ACT), Inc.* Retrieved April 20, 2012, from http://www.eric.ed.gov/contentdelivery/servlet/ERICServlet?accno=ED490828

American Library Association. (2006). Presidential Committee on Information Literacy. Retrieved August 4, 2009 from *http://www.ala.org/ala/mgrps/divs/acrl/publications/whitepapers/presidential.cfm* (Document ID: 126315).

Bloom B. S. (1956). *Taxonomy of Educational Objectives, Handbook I: The Cognitive Domain.* New York, NY: David McKay Co. Inc.

Caine, R. N., & Caine, G. (1991). *Teaching and the human brain.* Alexandria, VA: Association for Supervision and Curriculum Development.

Combs, J., Slate, J., Moore, G., Bustamante, R., Onwuegbuzie, A., & Edmonson, S. (2010). Gender Differences in College Preparedness: A Statewide Study. *Urban Review, 42*(5), 441–457. doi:10.1007/s11256-009-0138-x

Common Core State Standards Initiative. (2010a). *Common core state standards for English language arts & literacy in history/social studies, science, and technical subjects.* Washington, DC: National Governors Association Center for Best Practices and Council of Chief State School Officers. Retrieved February 5, 2012, from http://www.corestandards.org/assets/CCSSI_ELA%20Standards.pdf

Common Core State Standards Initiative. (2010b). *Common core state standards for mathematics.* Washington, DC: National Governors Association Center for Best Practices and Council of Chief State School Officers. Retrieved April 26, 2012, from http://www.corestandards.org/assets/CCSSI_Math%20Standards.pdf

Common Core State Standards Initiative. (2010c). *Common core state standards for English language arts & literacy in history/social studies, science, and technical subjects Appendix A: Research support key elements of the standards; Glossary of terms.* Washington, DC: National Governors Association Center for Best Practices and Council of Chief State School Officers.

Retrieved April 20, 2012, from http://www.corestandards.org/assets/Appendix_A.pdf

Common Core State Standards Initiative. (2010d). *Common core state standards for English language arts & literacy in history/social studies, science, and technical subjects Appendix B: Text exemplars and sample performance tasks*. Washington, DC: National Governors Association Center for Best Practices and Council of Chief State School Officers. Retrieved April 26, 2012, from http://www.corestandards.org/assets/Appendix_B.pdf

Conboy, B. T., Sommerville, J. A., & Kuhl, P. K. (2008). Cognitive control factors in speech perception at 11 months. *Developmental Psychology, 44*(5), 1505–1512. doi:10.1037/a0012975

Concept mapping types of texts retrieved March 22, 2012, from *http://www.cheney268.com/learning/organizers/TypesText.htm*

Costa, A. (2011). *Costa's Levels of Inquiry*. Retrieved March 20, 2012 from *www.fresno.k12.ca.us/divdept/sscience/.../CostaQuestioning.pdf*

Covey, S. R. (1989). *The seven habits of highly effective people: Restoring the character of ethic*. New York, NY: Fireside.

Dahl, R. (1983). *Witches*. New York, NY: Scholastic, Inc.

Davies, A. (2000). *Making classroom assessment work*. Merville, B.C.: Connections Pub.

Disney, W. (1961). *The absent-minded professor*. Information retrieved July 14, 2012 from http://www.imdb.com/title/tt0054594

Dossett, D., & Burns, B. (2000). The development of children's knowledge of attention and resource allocation in single and dual tasks. *The Journal of Genetic Psychology, 161*(2), 216–234. Retrieved September 5, 2009, from Research Library. (Document ID: 54901844).

Dufour, R. & Eaker, R. (1998). Professional learning communities at work: Best practices for enhancing student achievement. Bloomington, Indiana: National Education Service.

Dweck, C. S. (2010). Even Geniuses Work Hard. *Educational Leadership, 68*(1), 16. Retrieved May 6, 2012 from *https://search.ebscohost.com/login.aspx?direct=true&db=f5h&AN=53491076&site=eds-live*

English, F. (2000). *Deciding what to teach and test* [Milenial ed.]. Thousand Oaks, CA: Corwin Press, Inc.

Fitzgerald, F. S. (1922). *Tales of the jazz age. The Curious Case of Benjamin Button*. Retrieved May 25, 2012 from *http://www.readbookonline.net/read/690/10628/*

Fox, M. (2001). *Reading magic: Why reading aloud to our children will change their lives forever*. Orlando, Florida: Harcourt.

Gladwell, M. (2008). *Outliers: The story of success*. New York: Little, Brown and Company.

Goldberg, M. F. (1990). Portrait of Madeline Hunter. *Educational Leadership, 47*(5), 41. Retrieved April 2, 2012 from *https://search.ebscohost.com/login.aspx?direct=true&db=f5h&AN=8525203&site=eds-live*

Gould, J. S., & Gould, E. J. (1999). Four square writing method: A unique approach to teaching basic writing skills (Gr. 1–3). Carthage, Illinois: Teaching & Learning Company.

Gould, J. S., & Gould, E. J. (2002). *Four square. The total writing classroom: A companion to the four square writing method* (Gr. 1–4). Carthage, Illinois: Teaching & Learning Company.

Hambright, W., & Franco, M. (2008). Living the "Tipping Point": Concurrent teacher leader and principal preparation. *Education, 129*(2), 267–273. Retrieved August 9, 2009, from Research Library. (Document ID: 1803412661).

Hunter, M. (1994). *Enhancing teaching*. New York, NY: Macmillan College Publishing Company.

Jones, S. M. (2011). Reading and Writing Strategies for the High School Student. *Virginia English Bulletin, 61*(2), 20–22. Retrieved May 6, 2012 from *http://search.ebscohost.com.ezproxy.apollolibrary.com/login.aspx?direct=true&db=ehh&AN=73796383&site=ehost-live*

Kingdon, C. (2005). Reflexivity: Not just a qualitative methodological research tool. *BrJMidwifery* 13; 622–627.

Kyndt, E., Dochy, F., Struyven, K., & Cascallar, E. (2011). The direct and indirect effect of motivation for learning on students' approaches to learning through the perceptions of workload and task complexity. *Higher Education Research & Development, 30*(2), 135–150. doi:10.1080/07294360.2010.501329

Lauer, S., & Yodanis, C. (2004, July). The international social survey programme (ISSP): A tool for teaching with an international perspective. *Teaching Sociology, 32*(3), 304–313. Retrieved August 4, 2009, from SocINDEX with Full Text database.

Lee, D. (2012). Genres, registers, text types, domains and styles: Clarifying the concepts and navigating the path through the BNC Jungle. Retrieved March 22, 2012, from *http://llt.msu.edu/vol5num3/pdf/lee.pdf*

Lee, H. (1960). *To kill a mockingbird*. New York, NY: HarperCollins, Publishers. *http://www.harpercollins.com/books/kill-mockingbird-harper-lee/?isbn=9780060935467*

Maiorana, V. P. (1995). *The analytical student: A whole learning study guide for high school and college students*. Bloomington, Indiana: EDINFO Press, Indiana University. Retrieved February 29, 2012 from *http://www.eric.ed.gov/ERICWebPortal/detail?accno=ED374395*

Marzano, R., Pickering, D., & Pollock, J. (2001). *Classroom instruction that works: Research-based strategies for increasing student achievement*. Alexandria, VA: Association for Supervision and Curriculum Development.

Marzano, R. J. (2004). *Building Background Knowledge for Academic Achievement: Research on what works in schools.* Alexandria, Virginia: Association for Supervision and Curriculum Development.

Meyer, K., & Kelley, M. (2007). Improving Homework in Adolescents with Attention-Deficit/Hyperactivity Disorder: Self vs. Parent Monitoring of Homework Behavior and Study Skills. *Child & Family Behavior Therapy, 29*(4), 25–42. *doi:10.1300/J019v29n04_02*

Mezuk, B., Bondarenko, I. , Smith, S., & Tucker, E. (2011). Impact of participating in a policy debate program on academic achievement: Evidence from the Chicago Urban Debate League. *Educational Research and Reviews 6*(9) pp. 622–635. Retrieved May 6th 2012 from *http://www.academicjournals.org/ERR*

Miller, S., Drill, K., & Behrstock, E. (2010). Meeting Teachers Half Way. *Phi Delta Kappan, 91*(7), 31. Retrieved June 4, 2011 from *http://web.ebscohost.com.ezproxy.apollolibrary.com*

MindEdge (2010). *Considering the whole part whole learning model.* Retrieved February 29, 2010 from *http://www.mindedge.com/MindEdge_WPW_White Paper.pdf*

Müller-Wienbergen, F., Müller, O., Seidel, S., & Becker, J. (2011). Leaving the beaten tracks in creative work—A design theory for systems that support convergent and divergent thinking. *Journal of the Association for Information Systems, 12*(11), 714–740. Retrieved March 29, 2012 *https://search.ebscohost.com/login.aspx?direct=true&db=bth&AN=71702708& site=eds-live*

Musgrove, (2006). The Real Reason Students Can't Write. *Inside Higher Ed.* Retrieved June 6, 2012, from *http://www.insidehighered.com/views/2006/04/ 28/musgrove*

National Association of Governors and the Council of Chief School Officers (2008). *Common core state standards for English language arts & literacy in history/social studies, science, and technical subjects.* Retrieved March 10, 2012 from *http://www.corestandards.org/*

National Commission on Writing in America's Schools and Colleges. (2006). *Writing and school reform: The neglected "r."* Retrieved from *www.host-collegeboard.com/advocacy/writing/publications.html*

Papert, S. (1980) *Mindstorms: Children, computers, and powerful ideas.* New York: Basic Books.

Pauk, W., Owens, R. J. Q. (2011). *How to study in college* (10th ed.). Boston, MA: Wadsworth, Cengage Learning. Chapter 10: Cornell Notes, see also *http://www.montgomerycollege.edu/Departments/enreadtp/Cornell.html*

Peters, B. (2011). Lessons about Writing to Learn from a University-High School Partnership. *WPA: Writing Program Administration—Journal of the*

Council of Writing Program Administrators, 34(2), 59–88. Retrieved May 6th, 2012 from *http://search.ebscohost.com.ezproxy.apollolibrary.com/login.aspx?direct=true&db=ehh&AN=61337084&site=ehost-live*

Poe, E. A. (1846). *Cask of Amontillado*. Retrieved June 16, 2012 from *www.bompacrazy.com/library/library/poe.../the_cask_of_amontillado.pdf*

Pohl, M. (2000). *Learning to Think, Thinking to Learn: Models and Strategies to Develop a Classroom Culture of Thinking*. Cheltenham, VIC.: Hawker Brownlow.

Reeves, D. (2007). *Ahead of the curve: The power of assessment to transform teaching and learning*. Bloomington, Indiana: Solution Tree Press.

Richland, L., Kornell, N., & Kao, L. (2009). The pretesting effect: do unsuccessful retrieval attempts enhance learning? *Journal of Experimental Psychology. Applied, 15*(3), 243–257. Retrieved from MEDLINE with Full Text database.

Rowe, M. B. (1974). Wait-time and rewards as instructional variables, their influence on language, logic, and fate control: Part one–Wait-time. *Journal of Research in Science Teaching, 11*, 81–94.

Rowe, M. B. (1987). Wait time: Slowing down may be a way of speeding up. *American Educator, 11*, 38–48.

Ruggiero, V. R. (2009). *The art of thinking: A guide to critical and creative thought*. New York: Longman.

Saxe, G. (1873). *The Poems of John Godfrey Saxe, Complete edition*; Boston: James R. Osgood and Company. Retrieved March 20, 2012 from *http://rack1.ul.cs.cmu.edu/is/saxe/doc.scn?fr=0&rp=http%3A%2F%2Frack1.ul.cs.cmu.edu%2Fis%2Fsaxe%2F&pg=4*

Schmoker, M. (2011). *Focus: Elevating the essentials to radically improve student learning*. Alexandria, VA: Association of Supervision and Curriculum Development.

Schmoker, M. (2006). *Results now: How we can achieve unprecedented improvements in teaching and learning*. Alexandria, VA: Association of Supervision and Curriculum Development.

Schroeder, K. (2006). Raising Writing Skills. *Education Digest, 72*(4), 74–75. Retrieved May 6, 2012 from *http://search.ebscohost.com.ezproxy.apollolibrary.com/login.aspx?direct=true&db=a9h&AN=23254027&site=ehost-live*

Silverstein, S. (1974). *Where the sidewalk ends*. New York, NY: HarperCollins Publishers.

Smith, C., & Cardaciotto, L. (2011). Is Active Learning Like Broccoli? Student Perceptions of Active Learning in Large Lecture Classes. *Journal of the Scholarship of Teaching and Learning, 11*(1), 53–61. Retrieved May 6th, 2012 from *https://search.ebscohost.com/login.aspx?direct=true&db=eric&AN=EJ915923&site=eds-live*

ain, M. (1896). *A Connecticut Yankee in King Arthur's Court*. New York, New York: Aerie Books.

Verne, J. (1864). *Journey to the Center of the Earth*. New York, New York: Aerie Books.

Wells, H. G. (1938). *The war of the worlds*. New York, New York: Aerie Books.

White, R. (1996). *Belle Prater's boy*. New York, New York: Bantam Double Day Dell Books for Young Readers.

White, T. H. (1939). *The Once and Future King*. New York, New York: Ace Books.

Wiggins, G., & McTighe, J. (1998). *Understanding by Design*. Alexandria, VA: Association for Supervision and Curriculum Development.

Williams, D., & Coles, L. (2007). Teachers' approaches to finding and using research evidence: An information literacy perspective. *Educational Research, 49*(2), 185–206. doi:10.1080/00131880701369719

Willingham, D. (2010). *Why don't students like school: A cognitive scientist answers questions about how the mind works and what it means for schools*. San Francisco, CA: Jossey-Bass.

Wolsey, T. D. (2010). Complexity in student writing: The relationship between the task and vocabulary uptake. *Literacy Research & Instruction, 49*(2), 194–208. doi:10.1080/19388070902947360

Zabel, D. (2004). A Reaction to Information Literacy and Higher Education. *Journal of Academic Librarianship, 30*(1), 17–21. Retrieved August 4, 2009, from Academic Search Complete database.

Zhang, M., Lundeberg, M., McConnell, T. J., Koehler, M. J., & Eberhardt, J. (2010). Using Questioning to Facilitate Discussion of Science Teaching Problems in Teacher Professional Development. *Interdisciplinary Journal of Problem-Based Learning, 4*(1), 57–82. *doi:10.1007/s10972-009-9161-8*